PRINCIPLES AND METHOD

IN THE STUDY OF

ENGLISH LITERATURE

T0382373

PRINCIPLES AND METHOD

IN THE STUDY OF

ENGLISH LITERATURE

by

WILLIAM MACPHERSON, M.A.

London Day Training College, University of London

NEW AND ENLARGED EDITION

CAMBRIDGE
AT THE UNIVERSITY PRESS

1919

CAMBRIDGE
UNIVERSITY PRESS

University Printing House, Cambridge CB2 8BS, United Kingdom

Cambridge University Press is part of the University of Cambridge.

It furthers the University's mission by disseminating knowledge in the pursuit of
education, learning and research at the highest international levels of excellence.

www.cambridge.org
Information on this title: www.cambridge.org/9781107505476

First edition 1908
Reprinted 1909
Second edition 1919
First published 1919
First paperback edition 2015

A catalogue record for this publication is available from the British Library

ISBN 978-1-107-50547-6 Paperback

PREFACE TO THE SECOND EDITION

THESE chapters are written primarily from a teacher's point of view. Their purpose is to describe and illustrate methods of study that follow naturally from the logical and psychological principles on which the teaching of English Literature should be based. The book is written with special reference to the requirements of pupils in Secondary and Continuation Schools; but since most of the principles and many of the methods described are capable of being applied, in their essence, to the teaching of English Literature at all stages it is hoped that the book will be of interest to teachers of every grade. No attempt has been made to deal with the study of English as a whole: principles and methods are described in their application only to the reading of authors. From an immediately practical standpoint, my chief aim has been to show how English Literature, as it appears in the work of the best writers, may be effectively studied and rightly appreciated. This is a theme of wide interest, and I trust that the book will prove helpful not only to teachers, but to readers generally who seek guidance in the study of English Literature.

In this edition the number of pages contained in the first edition has been more than doubled, a large amount of new subject-matter having been added. Chapters VII to XI are new, and some emendations and additions have been made in Chapters I to VI, which originally constituted the entire text of the book. The subjects treated in the new chapters are "The Study of Narrative Poetry," "The Study of Speeches," "The Descriptive Touch and Imagery in the Teaching of Literature," "Reading Aloud and Literary Appreciation," and "Suggestions for a Course of Study, with special reference to Advanced Courses."

My thanks are due to the Editor of *The Journal of Education*, who has kindly permitted me to make use of the following articles contributed by me to his columns: "The Psychologic Basis of Literary Study in Schools"; "The Place of Lyric Poetry in the Teaching of English Literature"; "The Descriptive Touch and Imagery in the Teaching of Literature"; "The Logic and Rhetoric of Speeches." I have also to thank Sir Henry Newbolt for permission to reproduce his poem, "He Fell Among Thieves," and Messrs Cassell & Co. for permission to quote passages from Stevenson's *The Black Arrow*.

W. M.

November, 1919.

CONTENTS

CHAPTER I.

THE LOGICAL AND PSYCHOLOGICAL BASIS OF
LITERARY STUDY IN SCHOOLS.

THERE are two fundamental points of view—the logical and the psychological—from which it is necessary that a teacher should regard the particular branch of study which he professes.

When it is said that the teacher should regard his subject from the logical point of view, it is meant that he should possess an adequate and coherent knowledge of its content and nature; and this involves a conscious recognition and logical classification of the distinctive elements that constitute his subject as an organised system and branch of study. The value to the teacher of such an orderly and arranged view of his subject is that it indicates to him the general directions that his teaching should take, and the results that he may hope to achieve.

When it is said that the teacher should regard his subject from the psychological point of view, it is meant that he should consider it not merely as a body of logically formulated and discriminated material, not merely as a surveyed and arranged result, but as

material resulting from mental processes which, in a
modified form, must be reproduced in the pupil's
experience : he must consider his subject-matter not
in itself, as an abstract and self-contained thing, but in
relation to the pupil, as a factor in the pupil's growing
experience.   He must have studied not only the particular branch of knowledge that he professes, but the
general stages of growth in the development of mind.
The value to the teacher of this point of view is that it
will guide him in the application of suitable methods of
teaching, and enable him to vary them according to
the particular stage of development of his pupils.

The logical point of view furnishes a firm basis of
procedure : it imparts to teaching that stability and
authority which results from the teacher's adequate
and coherent knowledge of his subject and its possibilities.   The psychological point of view modifies the
rigidity that would characterise a method based on a
purely logical consideration of the subject-matter: it
secures that flexibility and practicability which is
characteristic of sound method.

The two points of view are not opposed to one
another : rather each presupposes and is necessary to
the other.   While the logical point of view considers
a fixed result, the psychological point of view considers
the process that produces the result ; but a complete
understanding of the result necessitates the study of it
in relation to the process that leads to it; and a complete
understanding of the process necessitates the study of
it in the light of the result to which it leads.   The
teacher's knowledge of his subject-matter, then, is not
weakened and distracted, but, on the contrary, is

strengthened and unified, by the consideration of it from this two-fold point of view.

There are three aspects of Literature which govern any logical conception of it as a subject of study: we may look at it from the standpoint of its matter or content, and from the standpoint of its form, and from the standpoint of its imaginative atmosphere. In an abstract way these three aspects may be considered separately; but in actual literature they are never found apart, and they are essentially interconnected.

When logically analysed, the essential nature of the subject-matter or content of literature is found to be that it should deal with living reality, with some aspect or aspects of the universe which shall appeal to the reader as being real and vital. Literature includes within its scope the whole of experience—life in all its fulness and variety—the experience of all the people who have lived or might have lived or may live: there is no event, no state of mind, no phase of life which, treated in the appropriate manner, may not form part of its subject-matter. It is from this close relationship of literature to life that, for the ordinary reader, the chief interest and attraction of literature proceeds; and for the literary critic also this relationship is of the first importance. In the volume entitled *Appreciations, with an Essay on Style*, Mr Walter Pater has pointed out that the distinction between great art and good art depends immediately, "as regards literature at all events, not on its form, but on the matter.......It is on the quality of the matter it informs or controls, its compass, its variety, its alliance to great ends, or the depth of the note of revolt, or the largeness of hope in it, that the greatness of literary art depends, as *The Divine Comedy, Paradise Lost, Les Misérables, The English Bible*, are great art." A literary critic may be absorbed in observing and commenting upon features of diction and style; but his observations and comments will be valueless if he does not recognise that these features must be judged, not abstractly, in themselves, but in their relation to truth, in so far as they reflect life and reality. Thus Sainte-Beuve said: " I hold very little to literary opinions. Literary opinions hold very little place in my life and in my thoughts. What does occupy me seriously is life itself and the object of it." And again: "there is one word," said Maurice de Guérin, " which is the God of my imagination, the tyrant, I ought rather to say, that fascinates it, lures it onward, gives it work to do without ceasing, and will finally carry it I know not where; the word *life*."

The consideration of the formal aspect of literature as a subject of study may be said to include within its scope in the first place the structural form, and in the second place the language and diction, of literary works.

We have seen that the subject-matter of literature, dealing as it does with all the aspects of life, is varied, but at the same time the essence of it—its close relationship to life and reality—is always the same. So too the structural form of literature is varied: it differs in the lyric, in narrative and in epic poetry, in the drama, and in the novel; yet the essence of it is always one, and, when logically analysed, it is found to lie in the suitable adaptation of means to an end. In the producing of a work of art the artist's mind is dominated, consciously or sub-consciously, by an artistic end or purpose which moulds the work as a whole and in each of its parts. "In literary as in all other art," says Mr Walter Pater, in his *Essay on Style* (*op. cit.*), "structure is all-important, felt, or painfully missed, everywhere—that architectural conception of work which foresees the end in the beginning and never loses sight of it, and in every part is conscious of all the rest, till the last sentence does but, with undiminished vigour, unfold and justify the first." And this "literary architecture, if it is to be rich and expressive, involves not only foresight of the end in the beginning, but also development or growth of design in the process of execution, with many irregularities, surprises, and after-thoughts; the contingent as well as the necessary being subsumed under the unity of the whole."

Again, if we consider the form of literature in relation to the diction and language employed, the choice of words and the build of sentences and paragraphs, we find that here also the essential underlying principle is the adaptation of means to ends. The form of a literary work, alike in its general architectural design and in the details of language and diction, is moulded by, and must be essentially adapted to, the nature of its subject-matter. Thus if a poet had chosen for his theme events and deeds of a lofty nature, embodying the thought of an epoch or breathing the aspirations of a people, his work would fall naturally into the epic form. On the other hand, if he wished to express a single thought, his work would assume naturally such a rigidly limited poetic form as the sonnet. So too the diction of literature is moulded by its subject-matter:

the essence of literary diction is its adaptation of means to ends, its fitness and appropriateness as a means of expressing the subject-matter: in the highest literature the word and the idea are fused and united with absolute justice: the right word, the happy phrase, is struck out in the mind of the writer from contact with reality, as naturally as a spark of fire is struck from a flint. The varieties of literary diction are many: it may be clear, simple, idiomatic, involved, rugged, collo-quial, learned, terse, quaint, polished, ornate; but it must always be marked by the essential quality of fitness and truth.

The third element in literature which helps to form our logical conception of it as a subject of study is the element of imaginative atmosphere. Every work of creative literature is permeated by a distinctive imagi-native atmosphere. The artist's temperament and all his past experience have woven a variously coloured tissue through which he sees the world as bathed in a variety of distinct and blending hues—the charmed hues of imagination and fancy. The varieties of imaginative atmosphere, as found in creative litera-ture, are innumerable; and as it is the most refined and subtle expression of temperament and personality there is in it an incalculable element that cannot be analysed. Yet the general essence of it may be dis-covered, and it is always the same: like the essential principle underlying the outward form of literature, it too consists in the adaptation of means to an end, worked out here in obedience to a fine sense of aesthetic fitness and harmony. This sense of fitness will lead the artist to select this imaginative element, and to reject that, as being appropriate or inappropriate to his purpose; and the result will be unity of atmosphere. Just as the outward form of a literary work must be marked by unity in the midst of difference, by the harmonious adjustment of the different parts in relation to the whole, so too its inward spirit, its atmosphere, must be marked by harmony. And this harmony of atmosphere is not independent of the adaptation of means to ends in structure and diction: if there be no unity of form and little appropriateness of diction in a literary work there can be no unity of atmosphere. The nature of the subject-matter must be reflected throughout in the appropriate structure and diction and imaginative atmosphere. The three aspects of literature as a subject of study—its content, its form, and its appeal to the imagination—must always be considered as being in close and necessary relation to one another.

It has been said above that the subject-matter of literature is life and reality; and from this truth the teacher may draw the most important inference that the study of literature on the side of its subject-matter may be made valuable and interesting at *all* stages of the curriculum. It is sometimes asserted that literary study is of value to only a limited number of pupils, to those who are naturally gifted with an artistic temperament. But as we are all interested, or capable of interest, in life, so we are all capable of being interested in the study of literature from the side of its subject-matter. Art has been defined generally as being " an expression, satisfying and abiding, of the zest of life[1] "; and this is true in the sense that every artist in his

[1] *The Private Papers of Henry Ryecroft*, by George Gissing.

work must be inspired by "supreme enjoyment of some aspect of the world about him." But by such enjoyment everyone of us—even the lowest intelligence—is from time to time inspired; and whenever we experience this enjoyment—if we look upon a landscape and keenly feel its beauty, when we see amid a crowd a face that interests us and stirs us to a sense of what is in man, whenever in any way a spark of intimate thought or real feeling is struck in us by immediate contact with the world—we are then moved by an impulse which is essentially artistic, because inspired directly by life. In this sense, and with the limitation that few are gifted with the capacity for artistic expression, we all possess "the artistic temperament"; and it may be added that in the teaching of literature, if proper methods be adopted, the human interest of the study may be made to appeal to all our pupils, from the youngest to the oldest. Viewed from the standpoint of its subject-matter, the essential function of literature is to enlarge the scope of our ideas and sympathies, to enrich and develop our human nature, to teach us to see and appreciate rightly "the varied spectacle and drama of life"; and it is this function that gives to the study of literature universal validity, a firm standing at all stages of the curriculum.

A further important inference which the teacher may draw from the nature of the subject-matter of literature is that the study of it, as dealing with life and reality, is calculated not only to create and foster in the pupil a theoretic interest in life and its manifestations, but also to teach him how to live—it has

a distinct ethical value. Here we touch upon a wide
question, the complete discussion of which would in-
volve an examination of the fundamental principles
that determine the relation generally of Art to Ethics.
Into such a general discussion it is no part of our
present task to enter; but a few necessary conclusions
which have an important bearing on the teaching of
literature may be briefly stated. In the first place, it
seems obvious that into literature, the subject-matter
of which is as wide as the universe and life, an ethical
element must necessarily enter. This will be generally
admitted; but it may be asserted, on the principle of
"Art for Art's Sake," that the ethical element in
literature is essentially irrelevant and should be for the
educated critic a negligible quantity. To this it may
be replied that the teacher is concerned not with the
trained critic but with the immature student; nevertheless, apart from this consideration, and from the
standpoint of method, it is important that we should
form some idea of the meaning and value that belongs
to this principle of "Art for Art's sake." Since all
literature may be regarded as a reflection of life, the
principle cannot mean that literature is indifferent to
moral distinctions: these exist in the universe, and
therefore they must be reflected in literature. From
the teacher's point of view, an important truth that
would seem to be contained in the principle is the
negative truth that the end of literature, as of all art,
is not consciously ethical: its aim is not consciously
to teach or preach. Understood to that effect, the
principle indicates a valuable maxim of method: the
subject of literature belongs not to the domain of

Ethics but to that of Art, and so soon as it is used deliberately as a means of teaching morality the teacher has passed beyond his proper vocation and ceased to be a teacher of literature as literature. At the same time, the ethical element is always present in his subject-matter, and as there presented cannot but influence the minds and characters of his pupils. " Literature," says Mr John Morley[1], "consists of all the books—and they are not so many—where moral truth and human passion are touched with a certain largeness, sanity, and attraction of form. My notion of the literary student is one who through books explores the strange voyages of man's moral reason, the impulses of the human heart, the chances and changes that have overtaken human ideals of virtue and happiness, of conduct and manners, and the shifting fortunes of great conceptions of truth and virtue. Poets, dramatists, humorists, satirists, masters of fiction, the great preachers, the character-writers, the maxim-writers, the great political orators—they are all literature in so far as they teach us to know man and to know human nature. This is what makes literature, rightly sifted and selected and rightly studied, not the mere elegant trifling that it is so often and so erroneously supposed to be, but a proper instrument for a systematic training of the imagination and sympathies, and a genial and varied moral sensibility.......Literature is one of the instruments, and one of the most powerful instruments, for forming character, for giving us men and women armed with reason, braced by knowledge, clothed with steadfastness

[1] "On the Study of Literature," in *Studies in Literature* (Macmillan and Co.).

and courage, and inspired by that public spirit and
public virtue of which it has been well said that they
are the brightest ornaments of the mind of man."

The conception of the content of literature as being
thus related to life will give the teacher a firm belief
in his subject as being interesting and valuable to his
pupils at all stages; but taken in this connexion certain psychological considerations are important. At
every stage in the study of any subject, the selection
and grading of material must be in line with the pupil's
dominant directions of activity, and must not be determined merely from the logical point of view of the
adult, with reference to the logically distinguished
sections of a systematized subject of study.   The
pupil's experience of life has been small, and consequently care must be taken that the literature which he
studies reflects such aspects of life as he is capable of
understanding. The subject-matter that is read must be
varied according to the stage of development of the pupil:
if it be beyond his comprehension and range of sympathy the reading of it will be hopelessly barren and
uninteresting alike to teacher and pupil. Thus from
the age of eight to twelve the literature that is read
should deal generally with the lighter and more cheerful aspects of life: it may tell a story or deal with
action: the poetry that is studied should be musical:
and always the diction should be clear and simple; on
the other hand, whatever is gloomy or deeply reflective
or passionate in tone, with whatever is obscure or
complex in diction, should be avoided.

Coming now to the second aspect involved in a
logical conception of literature as a subject of study,

we have to ask: is it possible for a pupil of school age to study the structural form of literary works, and, if this possibility be granted, at what stage of the curriculum should such study begin?

It has been remarked above that the essence of structure lies in its adaptation of means to an end: there can be no coherent structure in a literary work apart from the operation of a moulding and governing idea which shall underlie the whole work and each of its parts in relation to the whole: in other words, it is of the essence of literary structure that it should bear the marks of organisation and system. Now, this conception of system is one which can have no real meaning for pupils below the age of twelve or thirteen years: before it can be in any degree understood, a pupil must possess some power of reasoning continuously and connectedly, he must be able to grasp mentally different threads of reason and consequence, and perceive their interrelations in a coherent whole. In the earlier stages of mental development a child is satisfied with the mere play of bodily and mental activity, underlying which there is no conscious or explicit motive or end. Only by degrees there comes to the growing consciousness some sense of cause and effect, or of the connexion between a certain course of action and a certain result, with a perception of the possibility of more permanent and objective ends than have hitherto occupied the attention. With the gradual increase of power, it becomes possible for the mind to distinguish between the sphere of natural or physical causation and the sphere of human action and thought as determined by a purpose or end. And as the mental development proceeds, there becomes possible the conception of a related system of cause and effect, of reason and consequence. When a pupil has reached the age of twelve or thirteen his powers of reasoning have developed sufficiently to enable him to comprehend relations of cause and effect, and the adaptation of means to an end, in a simple system. This indicates to the teacher that the study of structure in literature should not be begun before that age; and it affords to him a firm ground for believing that after that age the study of structure should form an essential part of the literary course. The movement of the intellect is instinctively onward towards coherence and system; and the study of structure in literature is one of the means by which that instinct may be satisfied and its development secured. If our teaching is to satisfy the nature of our pupils, from this time onwards we must offer a more systematic treatment of the subjects of study: we must emphazise wherever we can the relations of cause and effect, and the systematic adaptation of means to ends. In the later stages of the literature course, then, whatever be the particular class of literature that for the time being may constitute the object of study, be it poem or play, biography or essay or novel, the pupils should be required at suitable times to direct their attention to its structure, from the point of view of adaptation of means to ends: so that, after having read and considered it, they may be able to perceive it as a whole made up of parts skilfully arranged in such a manner as to produce the general effect at which the writer has aimed.

The circumstance that the essence of the form of

literature when regarded on the side of diction, no less
than when regarded on the side of architectural design,
is the adaptation of means to an end, a fine harmony
between the reality that is expressed and the manner
of its expression, indicates to us again that the formal
study of literary diction should not be attempted in
the junior classes. Speaking generally, the less verbal
criticism there is in the earlier stages of literature
teaching, the better and more effective will the teaching be; and at all stages of the teaching, whenever
the details of language are considered, the teacher
must consider these not in themselves, as isolated
features, but in their relation to the matter that is
expressed, or as producing a certain mental effect
aimed at by the writer. All the details in a work of
literary art are selected with a view to the attainment of an artistic end, and they should be studied in
relation to that end. In a letter written to Mr R. H.
Hutton with reference to her novel of *Romola*, George
Eliot bears striking testimony to this fact. "Perhaps,"
she remarks, " even a judge so discerning as yourself
could not infer from the artistic result how strict a
self-control and selection were exercised in the presentation of details. I believe there is scarcely a phrase, an
incident, an allusion, that did not gather its value to
me from its supposed subservience to my main artistic
objects."

It is frequently doubted whether pupils of school
age are able to appreciate rightly the effect of imaginative atmosphere in literature. Even if a favourable
view of the possibilities of literary study in schools be
taken, and it be admitted that the pupil may be taught

to perceive the "intellectual" qualities of literature—for instance, the logical qualities of coherence and continuity in a poem or treatise or essay—yet, it is said, he can by no means be trained to appreciate its "imaginative" or "aesthetic" qualities—its appeal to the imagination and its beauty of expression or of feeling. From this point of view, while it is admitted that the pupil may be taught to perceive some of the more prosaic qualities of literature, it is urged that he can have no vision of it in its higher, more poetic aspects.

In opposition to these opinions, it may be maintained that through the study of literature not only the pupil's intellect, but also his imagination and feelings—his whole human nature—may be trained and developed; and that there is in the curriculum no other subject so well fitted to achieve this particular result.

When it is said that possibly the harder and more logical qualities of a literary work may be utilized in teaching, but that its imaginative and aesthetic qualities cannot; when it is said that the study of literature in schools may possibly be a means of training a boy's intellect but cannot cultivate his imagination—to say this is to commit the serious psychological error of making an abstract separation of "mental faculties" where no real separation exists. There is no concrete state of mind that consists merely of reasoning or merely of imagination or merely of feeling: though we may distinguish between different aspects of consciousness, yet they do not operate apart from one another—the mind is a unity. And in a work of literary art the intellectual, the imaginative, and the emotional elements of human nature work in particularly close association and harmony: the artist puts *himself* into his work, himself considered not as a congeries of distinct "faculties," but as a whole-souled being, as compact of conception, of imagination, of feeling—each of his "faculties" being related to the other, and all blended and harmonized in the finished product of his art. No other subject included in the school curriculum presents the pupil with material that is so. "rammed with life"—so penetrated and inspired by the united action of all our faculties; and it is just this close association in it of intellect, imagination, and feeling that constitutes the special value of literature as a school study.

Remembering this connexion, and the fact that our faculties do not operate apart from one another, we may feel sure that, if we succeed in conveying to a pupil a sense of the intellectual qualities of literature, of the coherence and order and restraint that characterise a work of art, at the same time we shall have succeeded in conveying to him a sense of its imaginative qualities and its aesthetic value.

In other words, in the teaching of literature the imagination and the aesthetic nature may be cultivated *through the intellect.*

It is impossible to describe briefly what the distinctive function of imagination in literature is; but perhaps the best description in general terms would be to say that its function is to inspire atmosphere—an appropriate medium in which the creations of the artist may live and move. Atmosphere, it may be said, is the very life-breath of all literature (and of all art), just as it is of our material existence, and it may be admitted that only in so far as a pupil is inspired with the atmosphere of a book is the teaching of literature quite successful.   If it be said that the imagination refuses to be coerced, and that therefore it is impossible to compel a pupil to breathe the atmosphere of literature, the reply may be made that in reality there exists no necessity for such compulsion; that just as, in the material world, given the necessary bodily organs, we cannot but breathe the atmosphere of the place in which we are, so, too, in the world of literature, given intellectual comprehension of the book that we are reading, we simply cannot help breathing its imaginative atmosphere.

It is the more special function of the intellect in creative literature, to impart suitable form and design to a work, so that the exposition of its subject-matter may be marked by continuity, coherence, and unity. If a pupil shall have been led to perceive this unity of thought and structure in an imaginative work, he will have been brought a considerable way towards feeling the correspondent harmony of atmosphere.

Suppose, for instance, that a class is reading one of Shakespeare's plays, in all of which there appears the greatest complexity, while at the same time amid the diversity there is an underlying unity which serves as link of connexion throughout.   This unity of thought a pupil should be brought to see in each of the details that it governs; it will be seen often in those details that apparently are most irrelevant to the main issue. Thus, in *As You Like It*, the lyrics with which the speeches are interspersed would seem, on a first view, to be quite unrelated to the main idea of the piece.   Yet

M.   2 they are not really so.   Take the first verse of Amiens's song:

> Blow, blow, thou winter wind!
> Thou art not so unkind
>   As man's ingratitude;
> Thy tooth is not so keen,
> Because thou art not so seen,
>   Although thy breath be rude.
> Heigh-ho! sing heigh-ho! unto the green holly:
> Most friendship is feigning, most loving mere folly.
>   Then heigh-ho the holly!
>   This life is most jolly.

Than this lyric what could seem more spontaneous, purposeless, artless?   Yet throughout it, appearing in each sentence, there runs a thought that is intimately connected with the "plot" of the play—the song, one may say, so far as its matter goes, being a commentary on the banishment of the Duke, a contrast of his former with his present condition.   Now, a pupil who had been led to perceive this connexion, as regards its thought, of the song with the story, with the play as a whole, could not but feel—though perhaps quite unconsciously— how finely the atmosphere or spirit of the song accords with the atmosphere or spirit of the play: his imaginative and aesthetic nature as well as his intellect would be touched.

Suppose, again, that a class is about to study Goldsmith's poem, "The Deserted Village."   By his own previous study, the teacher himself will have realized that the spirit of this poem is in many respects of an intimately personal kind, significant of the circumstances of the poet's life and the conditions of his character; and with these circumstances and conditions the pupils, if they are to breathe freely and fully of the atmosphere of the "deserted village," must have previously been made acquainted: their imaginative and aesthetic nature may be reached through the understanding.   As a step, then, preliminary to the reading of the poem, and taken with a view to inducing in the pupils the right mental state, the teacher may begin by describing, in an easy conversational manner, such circumstances of Goldsmith's life and character as find expression in the spirit of the poem.   In the course of this narration the teacher will, wherever possible, quote by way of illustration any lines that may seem to him to breathe the essentially characteristic feeling of the poem.   Goldsmith, as a boy, was educated at Lissoy, a small village in Ireland, with which the "deserted village" of which he writes has generally been identified.   After he left Lissoy his life ran a somewhat troubled and erratic course.   He was of a careless and improvident disposition, which frequently led him into financial difficulties. He tried various means of earning a livelihood, and at length settled down as a writer in London.   While struggling to achieve success in his calling, in the midst of the bustle and noise of the London streets, he thinks with pleasure and longing of the quiet village where he had spent his boyhood.   The thought of the peaceful beauty of its scenes, contrasted with the struggle and the squalid environment of his later life in London, stirs in him a wistful regret and a deeper sense of the simple pleasures of country life.   Such illustrative lines as the following may be quoted:

> In all my wand'rings round this world of care,
> In all my griefs—and God has given my share—
> I still had hopes, my latest hours to crown,
> Amidst these humble bowers to lay me down.

2—2

Or, again, the lines beginning

> O blest retirement, friend to life's decline,
> Retreats from care, that never must be mine!

The poet's kind and generous nature and his own hard fight with poverty lead him to sympathise with the poor and lowly, and the poem is permeated with this feeling. The scenes and the characters with which Goldsmith had been familiar in his boyhood are drawn with a sympathetic touch. The teacher's first aim will be, by dwelling on these and kindred themes, to suggest to his pupils the mental atmosphere of the poem. The next step in the teaching will consist in detailed reading by the class, in the course of which the logical connexion and sequence of thought in the successive parts of the poem will be shown, and words and phrases will be explained with a view to making the ideas and images more clear and vivid. All through the teaching the direct appeal of the teacher is to the pupil's understanding; for, as has been remarked above, if a poem (or any work of art) is thoroughly understood by a class, its atmosphere or life-spirit will be breathed, and the highest aim of literature teaching as such will then have been realized.

When a reader breathes the imaginative spirit that suffuses a work of literary art, the mental result is the production of aesthetic pleasure. Now, a distinctive characteristic of aesthetic pleasure is its essential objectivity: that is to say, it is inherently related to the object which calls it forth. Before an object can produce aesthetic satisfaction, the mind must go through the intellectual process of perceiving it in certain relations. The teacher's task, then, in cultivating the pupil's aesthetic sensibility, is to present the object in those relations which form the intellectual basis of its imaginative and aesthetic appeal: he must *intellectualise*, as it were, for the pupil, or objectify for him in its mental relations, the imaginative atmosphere of a literary work. It is only in this sense that there can be said to be any *teaching* of literature on its imaginative and aesthetic side. It is sometimes said that the exercise of the intellectual activities is likely to destroy emotion and kill aesthetic pleasure. But this is not so: so far from this being the case, an essential condition of aesthetic satisfaction is intellectual comprehension of the object which gives pleasure. The imagination and feelings are trained not directly—from the nature of the case such direct training would seem to be impossible—but indirectly, through the intellect. And no subject is so well adapted as is literature to the task of so training them, because there is no other subject in which the qualities of imagination and feeling together are so predominant, or where they are so closely interwoven with the intellectual fibre of the matter taught.

CHAPTER II.

GENERAL METHOD.

THE first reading of a literary work in class should have for its main object the general comprehension of the subject-matter. The book should be read as rapidly as is consistent with adequate comprehension, in order that the subject-matter may present itself to the pupil as a continuous and connected whole. As the reading proceeds, the teacher will pause at convenient places, and ask such questions as may suggest to the pupils the essential meaning and relations of the successive passages. The questioning may be guided by three main considerations now to be kept uppermost in the pupils' minds. When incidents are being narrated, the important question to be considered is, "What is happening?" When objects are described, the question may take the form, "What is the pictorial effect produced, What do you see?" When ideas are stated, the question may be asked, "What is the meaning?" If a passage possesses a specially human interest, dealing with life in those of its spectacular or dramatic or moral aspects which the pupil is capable of understanding, the questioning may

aim at the illumination of the passage in those aspects:
the pupil's interest in life may thus be brightened and
deepened, and he may be induced to think and reason
for himself regarding human character and motive.
The study of a passage in literature with a view to the
elucidation of its human interest may be said to correspond to an object-lesson in an elementary course, or an
experimental lesson in physics or chemistry in a more
advanced curriculum. It is an experiment in human-
istic investigation, as the latter is in scientific investigation. Just as, after an experiment in physics or
chemistry has been performed, a boy may be asked to
explain the inferences to be drawn from it regarding
the natural world, so in literary study he may be asked to
explain, regarding the world of thought and feeling, the
inferences to be drawn from a passage or "experiment"
in literature. From the answers received the teacher
will come to know his pupils more intimately, will be
able to gauge more accurately their quickness of understanding and sympathy, their capacity for thought and
feeling.

In addition to the oral work, written exercises (to
be done either at home or in class) may be set. The
pupils may be required at suitable intervals to summarize the content of the book, and, on the conclusion
of the first reading, to write in as few words as possible
an account of the essential theme set forth in the work
as a whole. Suitable passages of poetry may be set for
paraphrase; the meaning of pregnant prose sentences
may be expressed more fully; and picturesque characters and scenes may be described in the pupil's own
words.

Side by side with, and in close relation to, the study of the content, in the senior classes, the study of structure may proceed. The essence of literary structure is that it is marked by unity in difference, by the adaptation of means to the attainment of an artistic end. Different, though interrelated, phases of the subject under treatment may be presented: there may be a main theme, and a larger or smaller number of minor themes according to the greater or less complexity of the structure; and all these will be related to one another and to the whole scheme by an underlying artistic purpose. The teacher's object here is to secure that the pupil perceives the different aspects of the structure as distinct from one another, and also as related and unified in a complete whole. Thus, in a novel or a drama, the various threads of the plot are woven in the first portion of the work; and the teacher's questioning should enable the pupil to distinguish and describe these as they are introduced: at the end of a chapter or a scene the questions may be asked—With which thread of the plot is this chapter or scene mainly concerned? and: Is any other thread introduced, with a view to maintaining the reader's interest in it and keeping before his mind the interrelations of the various threads?

The structural form of a literary work may often be conveniently shown by a tabular scheme, the different parts of the structure being represented in parallel columns[1]. Each column may be headed by a title which

[1] See *The Teaching of English in the Elementary and Secondary School*. By Percival Chubb. New York: The Macmillan Company, 1905. Page 282.

shall express briefly the subject-matter of its section;
and the chief details to be included under it may be
written below the title.

Scheme for the Study of Structure.

Theme (or Thread) 1	Theme (or Thread) 2	Theme (or Thread) 3

In such a tabular form the distinct development of
the different aspects of the subject-matter will be clearly
seen; and at the end of the form there may be added
a statement dealing with the interrelations of the
sections.

Many teachers may consider this kind of exercise to
be too formal, but at least the principle underlying it
is sound and should be kept in view in any more informal and conversational study of structure.

The main principle to be emphasized is the close
connexion between content and structure in literature.
The study of structural form cannot be carried on apart
from the study of the subject-matter which is formulated
by it; nor can the content of literature be fully appreciated apart from the form which defines it.

It follows from this circumstance that in the senior
classes—whenever the study of structure and a more
adequate study of the content of literature are aimed
at—most of the books that are read should be
complete in themselves, showing a developed artistic
structure.

The question is often asked whether complete texts or selected passages should be read in class. There is room, perhaps, at different times, for the use of both kinds. In senior classes books of selections are useful for teaching the history of literature and for applying the comparative method; but, since they afford no means for the adequate study of literary structure and atmosphere, their use should always be accompanied by the study of works forming complete wholes. So far as the junior classes are concerned, it is possible to say more in favour of the use of selections. In these classes we cannot hope to gain for the pupils all that is to be derived from the study of literature : their attention is to be directed mainly to the content of what is read, and this may be done when selected passages are used. Indeed, it may be claimed that here selections possess an advantage over complete texts, in that a volume of good selections may reflect more varied aspects of life ; and every teacher knows how necessary variety of subject-matter is in order that the interest of young pupils may be sustained[1].

After a book has been read with a view to the general comprehension of the subject-matter and structure, it may be re-read—this time with a view to the study of linguistic details and style.

The old method of studying our literary master-pieces in schools proceeded on the idea that they were to be used mainly as a means of imparting to pupils information relating to grammar, philology, or literary expression : the matter or content of literature was

[1] See note at end of chapter, p. 38.

neglected in favour of the study of formal details. Within recent years there has set in a reaction against this mode of treatment, and the tendency of "the reformed method" is to emphasize the importance of studying the content of literary works. There can be no doubt that this tendency is in a right direction: as was remarked in the preceding chapter, the aim which gives validity to the teaching of literature at every stage of the curriculum is the humanizing and enriching of the pupil's nature, through the study of the subject-matter; and that aim cannot be realized if the masterpieces of literature are used merely, or chiefly, as a medium for instruction in grammatical, philological, or literary detail. At the same time, we must be careful to take from literature, in the successive stages of the curriculum, all that the study of it is able to give; and since after the age of 12 or 13 a pupil may profitably make some study of the subject on the side of structural form and language, we must not indiscriminately all through the curriculum direct our pupils' attention exclusively to the content. We shall be confirmed in this opinion if we reflect that the content of literature is vitally interconnected with its form, and cannot be fully considered apart from it.

One of the most important points on which the teacher has to decide is the amount of detailed formal treatment that should be given. This will be determined partly by the nature and form of the book that is being studied, and partly by the stage of development of the pupil. There are certain classes of literature—for example, the novel—that are not well adapted for the exposition of linguistic and literary details. On

the other hand, there are some works—as the dramas
of Shakespeare—that are specially well adapted for such
exposition. In classes of younger pupils the discussion
of linguistic or literary details should be avoided. An
important general principle which may guide the
teacher in this matter is that detailed treatment is
desirable whenever it will add materially to the meaning
or force of a passage for the pupil. The formal features
of language and style must be studied in their relation
to the subject-matter and the artistic objects of the
writer: when they are so studied, they cease to be
merely formal, and become pregnant with meaning and
interest. For example, Milton frequently employs
words in unusual senses according to the meaning of the
Latin or other words from which they are derived (e.g.
"horrid" = bristling, in "a horrid front," *Paradise Lost*, I.
563); in such case the derivations of the words should be
explained as throwing light on the meaning. Again, if
a class were reading Tennyson's *Coming of Arthur*,
and came to the words:

> And on the spike that split the mother's heart
> Spitting the child,

the teacher might first ask what classes of vowel and
consonant sounds predominate in the words; and he
would then proceed to ask what mental effect is
produced by their use. If, in the reading of these lines,
a pupil were made to feel the impression of short and
sharp action produced by the succession of short vowel
sounds and sharp consonant sounds, his appreciation of
the content and force of the passage would be greatly
heightened. Similarly, the content of these lines from
The Lotos-Eaters—

Is there any peace
In ever climbing up the climbing wave?

would be enlarged for the pupil if he felt that the repetition of the word "climbing" suggests a sense of repeated effort and continuous toil, opposed to the idea of peace mentioned in the first line.

Throughout the second reading of a literary work, the pupils should be required as far as possible to discover for themselves the significance of the linguistic or literary details selected for comment. The method of teaching literature should be largely heuristic; and this being so, it is desirable in most cases that the text-books used in class should contain few "notes." The typical old-fashioned school-edition of an English author was, like Hamlet's marriage tables, "coldly furnished forth" with stale fragments of grammatical and philological information. Much of this information, regarded in the light of the principle that only such details should be selected for notice as will add to the meaning or the artistic conception of a passage, is seen to be misplaced and superfluous; and for the remainder, much of the material that is thus supplied by the editor may more profitably be acquired by the pupil's own researches.

The oral work connected with the detailed study may be supplemented by written exercises mainly revisional in character. At intervals, after a certain amount of ground has been covered, written answers may be required which will summarize the significant details that have been studied. For example, an exercise might be set on the words that had been commented upon in the reading of a certain number of

pages. The pupil would be asked to write down, with
adequate references to pages or lines, such features as
obsolete words, words that have changed in meaning,
derivations, explanations of meaning, or any other verbal
characteristics that might have been noticed in the
course of the class-teaching.

Notes on Words.

Meanings	Words changed in meaning	Derivations	Obsolete words	Page, etc.

Another exercise might have for its subject the
figures of speech that had been commented upon in
class.

Notes on Figures of Speech.

Similes	Metaphors	Antithesis	Climax	Exclamation	Page, etc.

Other exercises might deal with grammatical peculiarities, or with metrical characteristics, or with
allusions and their explanations. The writing of such

exercises enables the pupil to make and classify his own notes, which, as thus formulated, will be infinitely more valuable to him than similar notes that he might find supplied in a text-book.

Before the second reading in class is begun, the teacher should ask himself two questions, the answers to which will determine to a large extent the course of his later teaching. In the first place, he should ask himself: What is the main theme of the book? The answer given to this question will guide him in the selection of the literary details to be noted in the course of the second reading. The diction and tone of particular passages will be remarked when they are in harmony with, or show in a clearer light, the content and artistic aims of the book. The second question to be asked is: What is the essential spirit or atmosphere of the book? The answer given will guide the teacher in the selection of details to which the pupils' attention must be called in order that they may appreciate rightly the imaginative atmosphere of the book.

The effect of atmosphere in a literary work, when it is regarded intellectually and objectively (as it must be so far as practical teaching is concerned), is in many instances seen to be produced gradually through an accumulation of suitable details which are selected, consciously or sub-consciously, in obedience to the writer's artistic sense. It is the teacher's business so to present these details to the pupil's intellect as to assist him to recreate imaginatively for himself the characteristic atmosphere of the book. Suppose, for example, that a class were reading Shakespeare's *As*

You Like It. This play is marked by a fresh joyous-
ness of spirit: it is an idyll of forest-life, full of the
feeling of the open air and nature.   The scene is the
Forest of Arden, where the banished Duke and a many
merry men with him live the free woodland life, and
fleet the time carelessly, "as they did in the golden
world."   The fresh, young spirit of this golden world
is breathed throughout, and finds expression in many
touches.   The allusions to the places and things seen
in the forest help to create and maintain the illusion of
out-of-door life.   We read of the lioness, the snake, and
the deer that inhabit the forest-glades.   The sequestered
stag seeks shelter near "an oak whose antique root
peeps out upon the brook."   Rosalind's cottage is " at
the tuft of olives here hard by."   The similes and metaphors that occur are frequently drawn from the analogy
of woodland sights.   Adversity is like the toad, which,
" ugly and venomous, wears yet a precious jewel in its
head."   Orlando, when Adam offers to serve him,
compares himself to a rotten tree—

> That cannot so much as a blossom yield
> In lieu of all thy pains and husbandry.

Adam's age is "as a lusty winter, frosty but kindly."
When Orlando demands food from the Duke, he
compares himself to a doe seeking food for its fawn.
Silvius says that his mistress's love is like a harvest, of
which he would be a humble gleaner—

> So holy and so perfect is my love,
> And I in such a poverty of grace,
> That I shall think it a most plenteous crop
> To glean the broken ears after the man
> That the main harvest reaps.

By a succession of such allusions a certain effect of atmosphere is created; and, if the pupil is made to perceive the relation of these details to the writer's artistic objects, he will be assisted to feel more keenly the imaginative charm of the comedy. So far as pupils of school age are concerned, the study of style and atmosphere must be carried on by reference to such concrete details as we have exemplified. Vague generalities, unsupported by details, regarding style and atmosphere, have no meaning or reality for young pupils. In the senior classes, however, at the conclusion of the second reading, pupils may be asked to describe generally the literary qualities of the work: its tone may be characterized as earnest, exalted, dreamy, flippant, cynical, cheerful, grave, melancholy, humorous, witty, pathetic; its diction as being simple, colloquial, elevated, polished, ornate, smooth, strong, or terse; or its style as being clear, direct, concise, or obscure and verbose; and always the literary qualities noted would be illustrated by particular examples taken from the book, and the appropriateness of the diction, style, and tone to the nature of the subject-matter and the writer's artistic objects would be shown.

The usefulness of the comparative method in the study of literature is now, so far as the literary critic is concerned, generally recognised. It is indeed a method that is indispensable to the work of criticism. Matthew Arnold, in his *Essays on Criticism*[1], remarks that in order to recognise the spirit of true poetry, we must study the writings of the great masters: we must know their finest lines and expressions, "and apply them as a

[1] Second series: *The Study of Poetry.*

touchstone to other poetry"—a few such passages, "if we
have tact and can use them, are enough even of themselves to keep clear and sound our judgments about
poetry, to save us from fallacious estimates of it, to
conduct us to a real estimate." Speaking more generally, Mr C. E. Vaughan says that "without reference,
express or implied, to other types of genius or to other
ways of treatment, it is impossible for criticism to take
a single step in definition either of an author, or a
movement, or a form of art....It is the highest achievement of modern criticism to have brought science and
order into the comparative method, and largely to have
widened its scope. In this sense, comparison *is* criticism; and to compare with increased intelligence, with
a clearer consciousness of the end in view, is to reform
criticism itself, to make it a keener weapon and more
effective for its purpose[1]."

While the value of the comparative method in
criticism is thus recognised, it cannot be said that, up
to this time, its due place has been accorded it in the
teaching of literature. The chief use that has been
made of it hitherto has been in the presenting of parallel
passages. This has valuable results, but a much wider
use of the comparative method may be made: it may
be applied to the interpretation not only of particular
passages, but of literary works as wholes. Thus we may
compare and contrast two works belonging to the same
department of literature and written by one writer, but
treating of different themes: for instance, two tragedies
or two comedies of Shakespeare, two of Tennyson's

[1] *English Literary Criticism: with an Introduction by C. E.
Vaughan.* London: Blackie and Son, 1896.

lyrics, two of Macaulay's essays, two of Scott's novels. Or we may compare and contrast two works belonging to the same department of literature but written by different writers and dealing with different themes: as an essay of Addison and an essay of Lamb, a comedy of Shakespeare and a comedy of Sheridan, a novel of Thackeray and a novel of Dickens. Or again, we may compare and contrast two works belonging to the same department of literature and dealing with the same or a similar subject, but written by different authors: for instance, Macaulay's essay on Addison and Thackeray's essay on the same subject.

The comparative method may be applied to literature in each of its aspects, to its subject-matter as well as its structural form and style; but it gives perhaps its most valuable results when it is used in the study of style. A sense of style may be best acquired by the comparison of works similar in kind but different in treatment. Examples illustrating various applications of the comparative method to literary works considered as wholes will be given in the following chapters. Here the method may be briefly illustrated by a contrast between the following short passages, which resemble one another generally in theme but differ widely in treatment:

(a)   A mighty mass of brick and smoke and shipping,
       Dirty and dusky, but as wide as eye
    Could reach—with here and there a sail just skipping
       In sight—then lost amidst the forestry
    Of masts;—a wilderness of steeples peeping
       On tip-toe through their sea-coal canopy;
    A huge dun cupola, like a foolscap crown
       On a fool's head—and there is London town!

BYRON.

3—2

(b)   Sonnet Composed on Westminster Bridge in
Early Morning.

Earth has not anything to show more fair :
   Dull would he be of soul who could pass by
   A sight so touching in its majesty.
The city now doth like a garment wear
The beauty of the morning ; silent, bare,
   Ships, towers, domes, theatres, and temples lie
   Open unto the field and to the sky,
All bright and glittering in the smokeless air.
Never did sun more beautifully steep,
   In his first splendour, valley, rock, or hill ;
Ne'er saw I, never felt, a calm so deep !
   The river glideth at his own sweet will :
Dear God ! the very houses seem asleep ;
And all that mighty heart is lying still !

Wordsworth.

Pupils may be asked to contrast, from the points of
view of thought, tone, and language respectively, the
pictures of London given in the above passages [1]. The
contrast may be set down either in parallel columns or
in the regular form of a theme.

TWO DESCRIPTIONS OF LONDON.

A Contrast.

1.   In Thought.

(a) Byron's stanza empha-
sizes the squalid aspects of London. The place is "a mighty
mass of brick and smoke," "dirty
and dusky." The steeples that
peep through the canopy of smoke
are like a dreary "wilderness."

(a) Wordsworth's sonnet em-
phasizes the brightness and beauty
of the scene. "Earth has not
anything to show more fair."
The sun has just risen, and the
buildings sleep in its calm light,
"all bright and glittering in the
smokeless air."

[1] This example is taken from *Composition for Schools and Colleges*,
by C. H. Maxwell, B.A.   Meiklejohn and Holden, 1904.   P. 134.

(b) Byron's stanza does not reflect spiritual and moral impressions, but merely the external aspect of the city.

(b) Wordsworth indicates the spiritual mood which the scene created. "Ne'er saw I, never felt, a calm so deep!" "Dull would he be of soul who could pass by A sight so touching in its majesty."

2. In Tone.

The tone of Byron's stanza is light and flippant, in harmony with the external and material aspects of the thought.

The tone of Wordsworth's poem is earnest and exalted, in harmony with the more spiritual aspect of the thought.

3. In Language and Style.

(a) The diction of Byron's stanza is not essentially poetic, but it is plain, direct, and effective. It expresses a picture in a few broad strokes. It is marked by a certain quality of conciseness and even of abruptness.

(a) The diction of Wordsworth's sonnet is essentially poetic. Inversion occurs in lines 2, 9, and 11, and the archaic forms "doth" and "glideth" may be noted. The style is smoother and more sequent than that of Byron's stanza.

(b) The figure of Personification is found throughout the stanza, but it is used in a semi-ironical manner. A sail "skips" into sight; the steeples "peep on tip-toe"; and London itself is personified as a fool wearing a "foolscap crown." Metaphor and Simile occur: such phrases as "the forestry of masts," "a wilderness of steeples," "like a foolscap crown on a fool's head," add to the conciseness and picturesqueness of the diction.

(b) Personification, Metaphor, and Simile are here used to produce vividness and poetic effect. The city, clothed in the beauty of the morning, is like a man wearing a beautiful garment. The sun and the river are endowed with the attributes of persons. The houses "seem asleep" in the sunshine.

(c) The verse is iambic pentameter, and flows lightly and

(c) The poem is written in regular sonnet-form. The open-

briskly. The easy flow of the stanza is aided by the extra-metrical syllable at the end of lines 1, 3, and 5. Line 7 is irregular. The closing couplet gives a pointed finish.

ing trochees of lines 2, 9, and 11 impart a vigorous impetus, and add emphasis to the expression. Line 6 contains six accents, and, to counterbalance, line 7 (which begins with two trochees) contains only four accents.

NOTE. With reference to the question whether it is advisable to read selected passages in class, it may be noted that in French Secondary Schools volumes of selections are very generally used. Referring to this practice in French schools, Miss Elizabeth Lee remarks: " Such books are very numerous and of great excellence. Sometimes in one volume of some 600 pages, extracts will be given from seventy-three authors of the seventeenth, eighteenth, and nineteenth centuries, beginning with Mathurin Régnier (d. 1613) and ending with Elisée Reclus (d. 1905)...Each extract is preceded by a short biographical notice (of fifteen to twenty lines), and a brief statement of what has led up to the selected passage, and followed by a *questionnaire*, in which among other things comparison is often suggested with passages by other writers on the same or a similar subject. Poetry, prose, and drama are included. Sometimes one century, for example the seventeenth, is illustrated ' par les textes.' The volume has 564 pages and includes extracts from forty-four authors (poets, prose writers, and dramatists), beginning with Maleherbe and ending with Saint-Simon. A few notes are printed at the foot of the page, to assist the comprehension and appreciation of the text. In books of selections the exact reference to the title and chapter of the whole work from which the extract is taken is always given."—(*The Teaching of Literature in French and German Secondary Schools.* By Elizabeth Lee. The English Association: Leaflet No. 18.)

CHAPTER III.

EVERY production of creative literature may be studied in relation to its content, structural form, diction, style and imaginative atmosphere. At the same time, the different kinds of literature vary in the relative value which they possess as enabling us to study these several aspects. Each form of literature, indeed, may be said to have its special place and function in class-instruction. Thus, while the novel, the narrative poem, the essay, the lyric, and the drama may all be used as means for the communication of certain general facts of language and style, each may also be used to do a special work which no other form can do so well.

The novel is at once the most characteristic and the most popular literary form of our time; and it is a form that is particularly well fitted to foster the interest of young pupils in the study of literature. Boys and girls are naturally fond of a story, and it is important that they should be taught to discriminate between the good and the bad in this form of writing: the prevalence of the "penny dreadful" and the cheap novelette shows that there is need of such teaching in our schools.

Among the different forms of literature, prose fiction demonstrates more simply and clearly than any other the close relationship of literature to life. In the novel, the romance, and the short story, the human interest is obviously predominant: they represent character and action, and the interplay of each upon the other. The drama also, it is true, represents action and character; but for young people the study of these through the reading of drama is more difficult: for, while the novelist explains more explicitly and fully the situations and characters with which he is concerned, the dramatist affords the reader little or no assistance in the way of interpretation or comment. Therefore, in class-instruction, the first study of a drama naturally comes some time after the first study of a romance or novel or short story. It is through the study of these forms that a pupil is most likely to become interested in literature generally as a means of interpreting life, and they thus possess a special and radical value in the teaching of English Literature. A passage from one of Hazlitt's critical studies, referring to the essay in its more familiar forms, may be taken as describing aptly some of the benefits to be derived from the study of fiction. "It makes familiar with the world of men and women, records their actions, assigns their motives, exhibits their whims, characterizes their pursuits in all their singular and endless variety, ridicules their absurdities, exposes their inconsistencies, 'holds the mirror up to nature, and shows the very age and body of the time, its form and pressure'; takes minutes of our dress, air,

looks, words, thoughts, and actions ; shows us what we
are, and what we are not; plays the whole game of
human life over before us, and by making us enlightened
spectators of its many-coloured scenes, enables us (if
possible) to become tolerably reasonable agents in the
one in which we have to perform a part. ' The art and
practic part of life is thus made the mistress of this
theoric.' It is the best and most natural course of study.
It is in morals and manners what the experimental is
in natural philosophy, as opposed to the dogmatical
method. It does not deal in sweeping clauses of pro-
scription or anathema, but in nice distinction and liberal
constructions....It does not try to prove all black or
all white as it wishes, but lays on the intermediate
colours (and most of them not unpleasing ones), as it
finds them blended with ' the web of our life, which is
of a mingled yarn, good and ill together.' It enquires
what human life is and has been, to show what it ought
to be. It follows it into courts and camps, into town
and country, into rustic sports and learned disputations,
into the various shades of prejudice or ignorance, of
refinement or barbarism, into its private haunts or
public pageants, into its weaknesses and littlenesses, its
professions and its practices : before it pretends to distinguish right from wrong, or one thing from another.
How, indeed, should it do otherwise ?

> Quid sit pulchrum, quid turpe, quid utile, quid non,—
> Plenius et melius Chrysippo et Crantore dicit.

'It tells what is honourable, what is base, what is
expedient, more amply and better than Chrysippus and
Crantor[1].' "

[1] Hazlitt : " On the Periodical Essayists."

The ethical quality of fiction is indicated by a later essayist, Vernon Lee, in the following passage : " While fiction—let us say at once, the novel—falls short of absolute achievement on one side, it is able to achieve much more, something quite unknown to the rest of the arts, on the other; and while it evades some of the laws of the merely aesthetical, it becomes liable to another set of necessities, the necessities of ethics. The novel has less value in art, but more importance in life. Emotional and scientific art...trains us to feel and comprehend—that is to say, to live....The novelists have, by playing upon our emotions, immensely increased the sensitiveness, the richness, of this living keyboard[1]."

Considered, again, as a product of art, fiction conforms to certain canons and conventions which should be studied. In the senior classes some attention should be devoted to the structure and artistic manipulation of the story. The " complication " and " disentanglement," the weaving and the unravelling of the threads of the plot, should be followed ; and the use noted of such devices as suspense, climax, and contrast. The special and characteristic value of the novel in the teaching of English Literature is not only that, as has been remarked above, from it a pupil may derive a broader and keener interest in life and literature, but also that he may learn wherein the art of telling a story consists, and the qualities that mark a story as it is told by our best writers. And as a medium whereby the art of structure in fiction may be studied, the short story possesses advantages which longer narratives

[1] Vernon Lee " On Novels," in *Baldwin: being Dialogues on Views and Aspirations*.

do not possess. Just as, in poetry, the lyric poem, because of its brevity, enables a pupil to study its structure with less effort than do the longer forms of poetry[1]; so here the structure of a short story may be more easily studied than that of a novel or romance: the plot is less complicated, and may be grasped as a whole at one reading and included in one view. Again, the study of short stories possesses the advantage that many varieties of narrative, differing in atmosphere and effect, may in a short space of time be studied consecutively and contrasted with one another.

Of the various forms of literature, fiction may be said to be the least of all adapted for giving instruction in grammatical and philological details, and in features of diction and style. Whether it be true or not that "the novel has less value in art, but more importance in life," it seems certain that for the teacher, at least, the primary consideration in the study of fiction should be its relation to life; and that relation is apt to be obscured if the pupil's attention is concentrated on grammatical or philological details. The treatment of fiction in class-teaching ought to be broad and rapid rather than detailed: at all stages it should deal with the content and structure rather than with linguistic and literary details, and always the human interest should rule paramount. It should be remembered, too, that in fiction questions of style and diction present themselves from a special point of view and should be so regarded. Thus such questions as the use of dialect, "local colour," descriptions of scenery, and the

---

[1] v. inf. Cap. V.

general style of the conversation, whether stiff and
bookish or easy and natural—questions that do not so
readily arise in the reading of other forms of literature—
may here be studied.

One defect that commonly marks the mode of
procedure adopted in the study of fiction is that much
more time than is desirable or necessary is spent in the
reading of a novel or romance in class. The book is
read aloud, from beginning to end, by the pupils; and
since usually a work of fiction is of considerable dimen-
sions, and only one or two lessons a week can be set
apart for the reading of it, often a whole year is occupied
in the perusal of one book. There are many objec-
tions to such a mode of procedure. One of the aims
which a teacher of literature sets before himself is to
initiate his pupils in a fairly wide course of reading;
and to the realization of this object the method under
consideration certainly does not conduce. A further
objection is that the method is unnatural and artificial.
The mode of reading books in school should not be
absolutely divorced from the mode in which books are
read out of school; and, as it is a familiar experience
that one is apt to lose interest in a novel the reading of
which extends over a long period, so too in schools the
perusal of a work of fiction should be fairly rapid:
when it is extended over so long a period as a year,
interest is likely to evaporate. Again, such a lengthened
reading in class is unnecessary, because, if a suitable
work shall have been selected, the majority of the pupils
will on their own initiative read through it in a few
weeks. And again, since, as has been remarked above,
the novel is a form of literature which is not so well

adapted for the giving of instruction in minute details of language and style, the amount of time to be spent on detailed explanation is thereby lessened. For these reasons it may be concluded that to a great extent the actual reading of a novel should be done by the pupils outside of class-hours. The teacher's work should be directed towards securing, by proper guidance and help, that the pupils' reading is done intelligently. His first object will be to see that they follow coherently the gradual development of the plot and structure ; he may afterwards direct their attention to the characters, and to the methods of characterization employed by the author ; and lastly, if he thinks fit, he may discuss questions of diction and style.

The successive parts of the story may be prescribed to be read, out of school-hours, week by week, until the whole has been perused. At suitable intervals the pupils may be required to hand in a written exercise

Stevenson's " The Black Arrow."

PLOT AND STRUCTURE.

1. *The Black Arrow*	2. *Dick Shelton and Joanna Sedley*	3. *Sir Daniel and the Yorkists and Lancastrians*

that shall summarise briefly the course of the story. The different threads of the plot may be traced in parallel columns, mention being made in each column of the various events connected with one particular thread. For example, if Stevenson's *The Black Arrow* were being read, the exercise might appear with the following headings :—(1) The Black Arrow ; (2) Dick Shelton and Joanna Sedley ; (3) Sir Daniel and the Yorkists and Lancastrians. (See the scheme given on p. 45.) The first column would indicate the incidents in which the band of The Black Arrow takes part, the second the adventures of the hero and heroine, and the third the historical setting of the tale.

The reading of the story having been accomplished, a general review of the plot and structure may be made. Questions such as the following might be raised : How does the book derive its title ? Is the title suitable, and if so, why ? Is there any point at which the interest of the tale reaches its height ? At what stage precisely is the climax reached ? Are there any minor "climaxes"? In *The Black Arrow* the climax is reached at the end of Book II. By that time the various threads of the plot have been interwoven ; and the remainder of the book shows the process of their unravelling. The hero, Dick Shelton, is engaged in two tasks : he is seeking to bring Sir Daniel Brackley to account for the murder of his father ; and he desires to marry Joanna Sedley. The first two Books of the story state the various events that lead up to the performance of these tasks. The mysterious murder of the hero's father, and Dick's consequent hostility to Sir Daniel, with his escape from the Moat-House, and his joining the band

of The Black Arrow, are the chief events connected with
the first task. The detention of Joanna Sedley by Sir
Daniel, and Dick's determination to rescue and marry
her, are the chief points connected with the second task.
In Book III the unravelling of the plot is commenced.
The reader's interest is sustained by the unsuccessful
result of the attempt to rescue Joanna. Book IV
describes the frustration of the scheme to wed Joanna
to Lord Shoreby. Book V brings Sir Daniel to his last
account, and ends with the marriage of the hero and
heroine. The title of the book is justified because of
the important part which the fatal Black Arrow plays
in the development of the plot. Lord Shoreby falls dead
before the altar, pierced by the Black Arrow, when he
is about to be wedded to Joanna; and thus there is
removed an obstacle in the way of a happy issue.
Later, Sir Daniel, as he stands face to face with Dick in
the forest, is shot through the heart by the Black Arrow:
the happiness of the hero and heroine is now secured,
and the tale is told.

When the plot and structure of the narrative have
been sufficiently studied, the pupils' attention should be
directed to the characters. Here again the tabular
form of exercise may be advantageously used. The
pupils may be required to set down in parallel columns
the names of the characters, the qualities that they display in thought and action, and the passages that may
be quoted to illustrate these qualities. The headings of
the different columns would then be: (1) Name,
(2) Characterization, (3) Illustrations, (4) References.
In the case of *The Black Arrow*, the exercise might be
begun as follows:

Stevenson's " The Black Arrow."

THE CHARACTERS.

Name	Characterization	Illustrations	References
Sir Daniel Brackley	(1) Unscrupulous.	The murder of Dick's father. His compelling Sir Oliver Oates to perjure himself.	Prologue, &c. II. 2, "By the mass! but ye shall swear."
	(2) Avaricious.	"The Knight of Tunstall was one who never rested from money-getting."— "I have a need for the lad, for I would sell his marriage."	I. 1. II. 2
	(3) Shifty and disloyal.	"I lie in Kettley until I have sure tidings of the war, and then ride to join me with the conquerors."	I. 1.
	(4) Courageous in battle, a good leader.	"His dash, his proved courage, his forethought for the soldiers' comfort," &c.	I. 1.

If this exercise should be considered to be of too formal a character, a similar result may be achieved by the pleasanter method of oral discussion, supplemented by the necessary references to the book.

The method of characterization, and the author's success in depicting the persons, should also be studied. Questions such as the following would be asked: Does the author describe the characters in detail when he introduces them, and habitually comment on their mode

of action, or rather does he make his comments brief
and leave the reader to draw his own conclusions from
the characters' speeches and actions ? In other words,
is the method of characterization, generally speaking,
analytic or dramatic ? Are the characters life-like ?
Do they act consistently all through the narrative ?
Is there any tendency to exaggeration of certain traits ?

After the characters, the style and diction of the
book may be considered. What epithets might be
applied to the style ? Is it direct, animated, brilliant,
artificial or dull, clear or confused ? Is dialect used ?
Are archaic forms used, and, if so, with what object ?
Is "local colour" employed ? Give examples of vividness of phrase or good passages of description. Is
there any humour ? Give instances. Is pathos a strong
feature ? Quote examples of pathetic passages.

It is a good plan to study successively novels that
may be conveniently compared and contrasted. In one
of the writer's classes the pupils read in succession Sir
Conan Doyle's *Micah Clarke* and Sir Walter Scott's
Old Mortality, romances which, while differing widely
in treatment, yet possess certain similarities as regards
their subject-matter. As the reading of the second
book, *Old Mortality*, proceeded, the pupils' attention
was directed to the resemblances and differences. Both
books deal with rebellions against established authority:
Micah Clarke with Monmouth's rebellion against James
as representing Roman Catholicism, *Old Mortality* with
the struggle of the Scottish Covenanters against the
Royalist forces as representing Episcopacy. The two
revolts were alike unsuccessful : in each of the tales
the hero, after the defeat of his party, is compelled to

M. 4

leave the country, and goes abroad to serve as a soldier
of fortune. While the story of *Micah Clarke*, however,
ends at this point, in *Old Mortality* the narrative is
continued after the hero has returned from exile to his
native land.   This difference in the subject-matter
corresponds with the greater complexity of structure
that marks Scott's romance. The plot of *Micah Clarke*
is simple, that of *Old Mortality* is complex. The former
runs on a single thread which links together the
adventures of one character—the hero—and his associ-
ates ; the latter runs along two main threads, the first
of which is connected with the fortunes of the hero,
Henry Morton, and the Covenanters, while the second,
running a distinct but parallel course throughout the
greater part of the story, and uniting with the other
only at the close, is connected with the fortunes of
Edith Bellenden and the Episcopalians.   In *Micah
Clarke* there is practically no love-interest : it is purely
a tale of adventure. In *Old Mortality* the main theme
is the love-story of the hero and the heroine, and the
hero's adventures are important chiefly in relation
to that theme. Hence, while the former tale ends
fittingly with Micah's departure from England, the
latter is continued until the hero and heroine are brought
together again and united. Structurally considered,
Micah Clarke consists in a series of loosely connected
chapters, each describing a separate adventure ; while
in *Old Mortality* the various incidents are connected
with one another by a central unifying theme. Corresponding with the greater complexity of its subject-
matter and structure, there is found in Scott's romance
a greater range and complexity of characterization. In

Micah Clarke the characters are nearly all fighting men and burghers: there are very few female characters, and those that do appear are merely sketched, not fully drawn. Scott's characters are taken from all classes, and his delineation of the Scottish peasantry, male and female, is especially vivid. The character of Henry Morton is much richer and more complex than that of Micah Clarke, and it develops fresh qualities as the story proceeds. Scott's Sergeant Bothwell and Conan Doyle's Decimus Saxon are both soldiers of fortune; but, while the latter is merely a soldier of fortune, a brave fighter with an eye ever to his own advantage, the former is shown as possessing qualities of heart which, despite his roughness of manner, endear him to the reader. A comparison of the two works leads to the general conclusion that the canvas of *Old Mortality* is wider in scope, and more varied in life and colour and atmosphere, than that of the later romance.

CHAPTER IV.

STUDY OF THE ESSAY.

THE characteristic function and place of the Essay in the teaching of English literature is defined by the circumstance that, of all the forms of literature, it is the most nearly related to the study of Composition. One of the most common exercises in English Composition consists in the writing of "essays"; and while these are not usually so long as the essays studied in the literature class, their composition is similar, and should be governed by the same general principles. As a form of literature, the essay is more within the creative powers of the pupil himself, more like what he himself is able to produce; and therefore, to a greater extent than the other forms of literature, it should be considered by the teacher with reference to the possibilities of its use as a model in composition.

An essay should first be read with a view to the discovery of its main theme and the author's particular point of view. A distinctive characteristic of the essay is that, in the treatment of the main theme, the writer selects such ideas or facts as are appropriate to a single point of view, and states these to the exclusion of others that may be quite as essentially connected with the subject. The art of discriminative selection is here especially operant, fundamentally important though it is in all the forms of composition; and through this form it may be most effectively studied. In this connexion, however, it is to be noted that in the more personal, intimate kind of essay-writing digressions from the main theme are permissible, and frequently occur. For example, in Charles Lamb's essay entitled "My First Play," the first paragraph introduces the main subject, pointing out to the reader the pit entrance to old Drury, where Lamb saw his first play; the second paragraph describes—somewhat discursively, but still relevantly to the main theme—the author's "godfather F.," who had sent the orders for the theatre; the third paragraph is digressive, and comments in Elia's kindly humorous manner on some of F.'s personal peculiarities; the fourth paragraph is again digressive, suggesting Lamb's feelings when he first set foot on a landed property left him by his god-father; the fifth paragraph reverts to the main theme. Such digressions are appropriate in the familiar style of essay, and often constitute a great part of its charm: they are, in Herrick's phrase, the "careless shoe-strings," the loosely flowing ribbons, the "neglected cuffs" of the essay, and the carelessness of their disposition may be more delightful to the reader than the carefulness of a more formal art.

> A cuff neglectful, and thereby
> Ribbons to flow confusedly;
> A winning wave, deserving note,
> In the tempestuous petticoat;
> A careless shoe-string, in whose tie
> I see a wild civility;
> Do more bewitch me, than when art
> Is too precise in every part.

When the first general reading of an essay has been concluded, the pupils may be called upon to write a coherent and adequate description of the main theme. The following may be given as an example of this form of exercise:

"*MY FIRST PLAY*"

(From "The Essays of Elia.")

Statement of the main theme and scope of the essay.

> After introducing the reader to the pit entrance of old Drury, Elia comments on some personal foibles of his godfather F., who had sent the orders for the play. Returning to the main theme, he carries the reader within the theatre, and describes the glamour surrounding a child's first glimpse of the stage—"no such pleasure has since visited me but in dreams." He then calls to memory his second and third plays; and, in conclusion, refers to the feelings with which he visited the theatre in his later life.

This exercise may be followed by a second, the object of which should be to present a more detailed outline of the essay: the pupil being asked to write down in their order the themes of the successive paragraphs—in other words, to make a précis of the essay. The great value of this form of exercise is now generally recognised: the making of a good précis involves the qualities of refined discrimination and close concentration, a logical faculty of grasping the essential points in the development of a theme.

"*MY FIRST PLAY*"

(From "The Essays of Elia").

Paragraph-Précis.

Par. 1.—The reader is conducted to the pit-entrance of old Drury Lane.

Par. 2.—The associations of Elia's godfather F. (who had sent the orders) with the theatre.

Par. 3.—Foibles of F.

Par. 4.—Through a legacy from his godfather, Elia experiences the elation of a landed proprietor.

Par. 5.—Interior of the theatre: waiting for the play.

Par. 6.—"The play's the thing": recollections of "Artaxerxes."

Par. 7.—Elia's recollections of his second play—"The Lady of the Manor."

Par. 8.—Recollections of his third play—"The Way of the World."

Par. 9.—Changed impressions: after an interval of six or seven years, Elia returns to the theatre a rationalist.

It should be added that, while most of the essays studied in schools may appropriately be analyzed in this manner, yet there are some which are not naturally adapted for such a strict written analysis. Some of the finest examples of the personal essay are marked throughout by an *abandon* which it would be a folly to try to confine in the form of a precis: in these the writer wanders fancy-free, from pole to pole of varied sentiment and idea, at the beck only of "random provocations." "We will have nothing said or done syllogistically this day," exclaims Elia in his essay on *All Fools' Day*, "remove those logical forms, waiter, that no gentleman break the tender shins of his apprehension stumbling across them "— in such cases it may be well that the teacher should for the nonce enact the part of Elia's waiter.

When the written exercises complementary to the first reading have been done, the essay should be re-read—this time with a view to the study of linguistic and literary details. It may be read paragraph by paragraph: a pause being made at the end of each for such questions and explanations as may be deemed necessary.

The paragraph should first be considered as a whole. In prose composition as a rule, each paragraph is marked by unity of subject and treatment: it deals consistently with one main theme. In the essay, however, as we have seen, digressions frequently occur: not only are whole paragraphs found 'to diverge from the general theme of the essay, but, within the paragraphs, sentences diverge from the particular paragraph-themes. At the end of a paragraph, the pupil may be asked to say whether it is marked by unity or lack of unity. If he has previously noted the paragraph-theme, he will have no difficulty in answering correctly: when a paragraph contains statements that are not related to its theme, its unity is thereby broken. The connexion between the successive paragraphs should also be observed. It may be explicit or implicit: it is explicit when one paragraph is linked to another by a special word or phrase—such as "thus," "in the next place," "we have now seen," or by the repetition of a word from the preceding paragraph: examples of such linked paragraphs should be pointed out by the pupil.

The sentences forming the paragraph should next be studied. The range of details that may be here noted is wide, and there is need for considerable care in the selection of questions and explanations. It is essential, however, that the meaning of the sentences should be understood by the pupils, and to that end any obscure allusions should be made clear. The teacher may be guided in his questioning also by the relation of the essay-form to the study of composition. In ordinary prose writing, the sentence, like the paragraph, should be a unity, should treat of only one subject: if it deals with more than one, it is apt to be involved in construction and obscure in meaning. In some cases, however, the want of unity in a sentence may not be a fault, and involution and obscurity may be designed to produce a distinct literary effect. Instances of want of unity in sentences may be pointed out by the pupil. The general character of the sentences, as shown through particular instances, may also be commented upon: notice may be taken of exceptionally long or short sentences and their structure as loose or periodic; and of balanced, antithetical, epigrammatic, exclamatory, or interrogative sentences: special emphasis being laid on the mental effects produced by these usages.

The words contained in the sentences may then be studied: the uses of unusual or obsolete words, technical

terms, foreign words, should be notice .. The derivations
of words should be made known when they impart
shades of meaning which would otherwise escape
observation. An important distinction in words, from
the writer's point of view, is that between specific and
general terms : both are necessary in every form of
composition, but while the former produce a more
vivid effect, and are found most frequently in descriptive
and narrative essays, the latter are expressive of abstract
ideas, and are especially useful in the treatment of
expository and reflective themes.

After the detailed reading of the essay, if it be held
desirable, written exercises of a revisional and summary
nature may be set. One exercise might deal with the
sentences of the essay, the pupils being asked to write
down (perhaps in tabular form) the particular features
that had been remarked ; or, in the case of the older
pupils, a more general statement might be required.
For example :

" MY FIRST PLAY "

(From " The Essays of Elia ").

Notes on the Sentences.

The length of the sentences in this essay is
effectively varied : there is a mixture of long and
short sentences of average length. The short sentences in the following passage express well the
sudden arrest of Elia's young consciousness when
the bell rings and the curtain rises :

" The orchestra lights at length arose, those
' fair Auroras ! ' Once the bell sounded. It was to

ring out once again—and, incapable of the anticipation, I reposed my shut eyes in a sort of resignation upon the maternal lap. It rang the second time. The curtain drew up—I was not past six years old —and the play was 'Artaxerxes'!"

A similar effect is produced in these sentences, descriptive of Elia's feelings after the curtain has risen :

"All feeling was absorbed in vision. Gorgeous vests, gardens, palaces, princesses, passed before me. I knew not players...."

The following is an instance of a long sentence :

"He is dead—and thus much I thought due to his memory, both for my first orders (little wondrous talismans !—slight keys, and insignificant to outward sight, but opening to me more than Arabian paradises !) and moreover, that by his testamentary beneficence I came into possession of the only landed property which I could ever call my own— situate near the roadway village of pleasant Pucke-ridge, in Hertfordshire."

The above quotation illustrates another feature of many of the sentences : their lack of strict unity ; and connected with this is the use of parentheses and exclamations, which occur frequently throughout the essay. Here is a characteristic sentence :

"The boxes at that time, full of well-dressed women of quality, projected over the pit ; and the pilasters reaching down were adorned with a glistering substance (I know not what) under glass (as it seemed), resembling—a homely fancy—but I judged it to be sugar-candy—yet, to my raised imagination, divested of its homelier qualities, it appeared a glorified candy !"

Antithesis and balance and epigram are occasionally found, but they are not prominent features: the following passage may be cited :

" I expected the same feelings to come again with the same occasion. But we differ from ourselves less at sixty and sixteen, than the latter does from six. In that interval what had I not lost ! At the first period I knew nothing, understood nothing, discriminated nothing. I felt all, loved all, wondered all—

Was nourished, I could not tell how—

I had left the temple a devotee, and was returned a rationalist. The same things were there materially; but the emblem, the reference, was gone ! "

Exercises may also be set on the allusions, quotations, and words contained in the essay. For example:

"MY FIRST PLAY."

Allusions and Quotations.

Par. 1.   Garrick's Drury.

Par. 2.   Sheridan.   Maria Linley.

Par. 3.   Ciceronian.   Seneca.   Varro.   "The parochial honours of St Andrew's."

Par. 4.   " Wondrous talismans !—slight keys, but opening to me more than Arabian paradises ! "

Par. 5.   "The plate prefixed to Troilus and Cressida, in Rowe's Shakespeare—the tent scene with Diomede." Those "fair Auroras" (an expression found in the first song in "Artaxerxes").

Par. 6.   Darius.   Persepolis.   Harlequin's Invasion.   The legend of St Denis.

Par. 7.   " The Lady of the Manor."   Rich.

Par. 8.   "The Way of the World."   The old Round
Church of the Templars.

Par. 9.   " Was nourished, I could not tell how "
(probably an echo from Walton's *Complete Angler*).   Mrs Siddons.

An explanatory note may be added after each
allusion or quotation.

" MY FIRST PLAY."

Notes on the Words.

1.   *Unfamiliar Words*[1].—prognosticate, **grandi-
loquent**, betwixt (*archaic*), pilasters, beshrew
(*archaic*), nonpareils, inhibited, beldams, **panta-
loonery.**

2.   *Words used in an unusual connexion*[1].—
" He arrived with his harmonious charge "; "these
distorted syllables "; "nothing but an agrarian can
restore it "; "monosyllabically elaborated"; " by his
testamentary beneficence "; "beshrew the uncom-
fortable manager "; "to my raised imagination ";
"upon a new stock"; "I was returned a rationalist";
"the primeval Motley "; "like some solemn tragic
passion."

3.   *Grammatical Peculiarities.*—"that by his
testamentary beneficence " &c. ("that " = because).
"situate" (= situated).   " an indispensable playhouse accompaniment in those days " (*playhouse,*
noun used as adjective).   "fruiteresses " (uncommon
feminine form).

4.   *Specific and general terms.*—The last sentences illustrate the use of general terms: e.g.

[1] Derivations may be appended in some cases.

"Comparison and retrospection soon yielded to the present attraction of the scene; and the theatre became to me, upon a new stock, the most delightful of recreations."

Finally, an exercise may be required which shall deal more generally with the essential spirit and style of the essay. This is a difficult exercise, and may be set only in the highest classes; but in every case the teacher himself should have previously studied the essay from the point of view here indicated: he will thereby gain valuable direction for his teaching. In the case of Lamb's essay on "My First Play," the exercise might take some such form as the following:

"MY FIRST PLAY."

Spirit and Style.

The essay is suffused throughout by an intimately personal spirit; it reveals to us the author both in his inner and his outer life: in his thoughts, fancies, and sentiments, and in his outward circumstances and social relationships. We have a glimpse of him first as a child, on a rainy afternoon in London, looking through the window at the rain splashing in the street. We see him then in the theatre, awaiting, with "breathless anticipations" and "raised imagination," the forthcoming spectacle, or rapt in the contemplation of the scenes and characters of the play. We are introduced by the way to his parents, as they sit at cards—"over a quadrille table"; and to them—post-haste from elopement—young Brinsley Sheridan enters with his bride. We smile at the oddities of the godfather, and of Elia himself, in his rôle of landed proprietor, striding—shall he confess the vanity?—with larger paces over his allotment of three quarters of an acre.

The structural form of the essay expresses appropriately its intimately personal spirit. The theme is not developed systematically or logically. The title of itself, considered in relation to the substance of the essay, shows this: it promises some account of Elia's first play, but the actual subject matter concerns not only the first, but the second, third, and later plays seen by the author. The second and third paragraphs digress from the main theme; and the course of the essay throughout resembles more the wayward flow of a familiar conversation than the studied development of a given theme.

The style of the essay is in harmony with the subject-matter and structural form. It is highly individual and characteristic. It possesses a strong savour of quaint humour, which makes itself felt partly through the use of uncommon but quaintly expressive conjunctions of words. Regarded generally, the style reflects qualities of the heart rather than of the intellect: it is stamped by a sympathetic humour and loving humanity, rather than by a sharp wit or penetrating intellect: hence some of the more purely intellectual features of style—such as antithesis, balance, and epigram—are not prominent in the essay.

It is a good plan to read the essays of several different writers consecutively, with a view to comparison and contrast. For instance, after an essay of Lamb's, one of Addison's might be studied. No. 335 of *The Spectator*, in which Addison describes Sir Roger de

Coverley's visit to the theatre, may be compared with Elia's essay on "My First Play." Here we have two essays dealing with similar subjects in similar styles. In one we read of the impressions of an unsophisticated old man—old in years, but young in heart and feeling, at the performance of a play; in the other we read of the impressions of an unsophisticated imaginative child. Both belong to the class of "familiar essays," but Addison's is differentiated from Lamb's in that, while it is not so intimately personal in tone, it has a superadded dramatic interest. No. 93 of *The Spectator*, again, may be contrasted with the essay on "My First Play." Here we have two essays dealing with entirely different subjects in different styles. Addison's paper in *The Spectator* deals with an abstract theme, "On Proper Methods of Employing Time," and is an example of the didactic essay. Its style may be contrasted to excellent effect with that of "My First Play": while the latter is suffused with feeling, the former is marked rather by intellectual qualities. Each of Addison's paragraphs forms a unity within itself, and many of them are explicitly linked to the preceding paragraph: it may be added that this mode of junction, superimposed by the intellect for the sake of greater clearness and more exact sequence, is more mechanical in kind than the fusion of paragraph to paragraph in the natural flow of feeling and thought, moving independently of external aids. Addison's sentences are marked by unity and clearness, and their most conspicuous feature is the extensive use of anti-thesis, balance, and epigram. The first sentences of the essay are characteristic: "We all of us complain of the shortness of time, saith Seneca, and yet have much more than we know what to do with. Our lives, says he, are spent either in doing nothing at all, or in doing nothing to the purpose, or in doing nothing that we ought to do. We are always complaining our days are few, and acting as though there would be no end of them." The words in Addison's essay are well-chosen and appropriately used; they are mostly words in common use, and have not the recondite quality of the vocabulary in Lamb's essay[1].

[1] Teachers will find in the undernoted volume material adapted to the application of the comparative method and of the general method of study indicated in this chapter :—*Prose Essays, arranged for Comparative Study, with Notes and Exercises*, by W. Macpherson, M.A. (Blackie and Son).

CHAPTER V.

THE STUDY OF LYRIC POETRY.

IT may be claimed as one of the advantages appertaining to the study of lyric poetry that through it as medium the importance of the element of structure in literature may be taught more easily than through any other literary form. The first lesson a pupil has to learn regarding structure is that a work of literary art should be pervaded by a certain unity: underlying all its details there must be implicitly present a central unity of feeling or thought and a corresponding harmony of atmosphere. It is the merit of a lyric poem, in this connexion, as compared with other forms of literature, that in it the reader may more easily perceive the central unity of its theme. This advantage lyric poetry possesses, in the first place, because it is, compared with other literary forms, brief in its expression, and is less overlaid with details; and secondly, because from its essential nature it aims at impressing on the reader's consciousness some single vivid idea or emotion—thus we find Mr Palgrave remarking in his preface to *The Golden Treasury* (*First*

Series) that "'lyrical' has been here held essentially to imply that each poem shall turn on some single thought, feeling, or situation." It is true, of course, that in every work of literary art, whatever be its kind, there must be amid a varying multiplicity of detail an underlying unity; and just in proportion as the perusal of the whole work produces this effect of unity is the work great as a product of art. Hence, in the higher stages of literature teaching, in all cases the structure of the literary works that are read will form an object of study. For example, it will be a valuable exercise for pupils who are reading a play of Shakespeare to trace the unity of plan, and the progressive development of that unity, throughout the play. Such an exercise, however, in the case of a drama will be a task of much greater difficulty and complexity than is involved in examining the structure of a lyric poem. A remark made by Mr Pater in his essay on "Shakespere's English Kings[1]" illustrates this point admirably. Lyric poetry, he says, "in spite of complex structure, often preserves the unity of a single passionate ejaculation"; whereas, in dramatic poetry, "especially to the reader, as distinguished from the spectator assisting at a theatrical performance, there must always be a sense of the effort necessary to keep the various parts from flying asunder, a sense of imperfect continuity." Mr Pater is here speaking of the difficulty which the adult reader finds in preserving the sense of unity amid the multiplicity of detail of a drama; and for the schoolboy the difficulty is much greater. The same difficulty, though in a lesser degree,

[1] *Appreciations: with an Essay on Style.* Macmillan.

will be met in the class-reading of a novel. It is only
when we come to the lyric that the study of structure
can be effectively carried on with an appreciably less
degree of effort; and the reason is that here we have
a form of literature the content of which may at one
reading be grasped as a whole and included in one
view. In a short space of time, in the course of a
single lesson, a complete product of literary art may be
studied and the interrelation of its different parts
clearly shown. It may be claimed, then, for lyric
poetry that it is a form of literature peculiarly well
adapted as an instrument for first introducing the
pupil to the study of structure and its importance as
an element in literary art.

So far we have been speaking of structure exclusively
in its relation to the subject-matter of literature, in
its signification as thought structure. It is impossible,
however, in considering any work of art, to make an
absolute separation between the subject-matter expressed and the manner of its expression. And in
lyric poetry this is pre-eminently the case. The
characteristic of a lyric is that in it not only the matter
—the particular feeling or idea expressed—but also the
manner—the mode of combination of words and phrases
and sentences, the metrical structure, the sound and
cadence of the verse—should proceed directly and
intimately from the personality of the author: in it
there should be a complete fusion between the
writer's personality and his subject alike on the side
of its matter and of its manner, each of which is to be
regarded as but an aspect of the other. For this
reason the relations that subsist between these two

sides of literary art, the matter and the manner, are more intimate, and may be more easily demonstrated, in the case of a lyric poem than in any other poetic form. As lyric poetry is now, on the side of its subject-matter, an instrument of many strings, expressive of all kinds of sentiment and thought, such an instrument is it too in the variety of its modes of expression: corresponding with the variety of the themes that it sounds there is a similar variety of metre and movement. Than lyric poetry, therefore, as represented in any of the many good anthologies now available, the teacher will find no better medium for impressing upon the pupil a sense of the intimate relation that subsists in literature between the matter expressed and the manner of its expression: for instance, in the reading of an anthology there will occur innumerable opportunities for explaining such points as the use and value in poetry, as formal aids to the expression of the subject-matter, of assonance, of onomatopœia, of alliteration, or the characteristic effects that are produced in particular poems by the employment of certain metres, and in a single poem by variations of metre within itself. And in drawing attention to these points the teacher will frequently employ the method of comparison[1]. Obvious differences in theme between two or more lyrics will lead to the observation of corresponding differences in sound and metre and movement, and the number of lyrics that may be studied within a short time makes possible a wide comparison of different types.

The reference that has just been made to the comparative method leads naturally to the consideration of a further point that defines the distinctive place of

[1] *v. A Book of Comparative Poetry*, edited by W. Macpherson, M.A. (Blackie and Son).

lyric poetry in the teaching of English literature. Lyric poems may be compared not only individually with one another, from the standpoint of their matter and of their manner, but also as falling into certain groups according to the periods in which they were written. The use of an anthology as a text-book ought to help us in our teaching of the history of literature. In the course of three or four terms' work an adequate selection of lyrics ranging from the Elizabethan period to our own, written by many different authors, and showing a wide variety of style, may be read—affording opportunities for the study of biographical and critical details concerning the authors, and for drawing comparisons between the different tendencies that have marked our literature at different epochs of its development. The usefulness of the anthology in this respect is suggested by Mr Palgrave in his preface to *The Golden Treasury* (*First Series*), where he tells us that " the poems have been distributed into Books corresponding (1) to the ninety years closing about 1616, (2) thence to 1700, (3) to 1800, (4) to the half century just ended. Or, looking at the poets who more or less give each portion its distinctive character, they might be called the Books of Shakespeare, Milton, Gray, and Wordsworth. The volume in this respect, so far as the limitations of its range allow, accurately reflects the natural growth and evolution of our Poetry." We have only to read Mr Palgrave's short but highly suggestive "Summaries" to perceive how easily the study of lyric poetry allies itself to the historical study of our literature.

But against this plan of using an anthology as a

means of correlating the teaching of literature with the teaching of literary history the objection may be urged that the chronological order in which the poems are given and the degree of difficulty which they present to the pupil do not correspond.

In reply to this objection, it may be admitted at once that, if an anthology is used as a means of illustrating the historical development of our literature, the poems that it includes must be read in chronological order; and it may be admitted, too, that in *The Golden Treasury*, for example, many of the lyrics given in the first part of the book are just those that are likely to present most difficulties to young pupils. Nevertheless, even in the First Book of the *Treasury*, there will be found many simple lyrics which may be understood and rightly appreciated by young pupils— such poems as Nos. 5, 15, 24, 27, 34, 42, 46, 47, 50, 51, 54. The teacher who uses *The Golden Treasury* as a text-book may use his discretion in selecting from each Book poems adapted to the age of his pupils; and, still preserving the chronological order, he may, if he will, combine the reading of the selected poems with the teaching of literary history. In a second review of the book the more difficult numbers may be read, and the correlated teaching of literary history will be elaborated.

As a further reply to the objection under consideration, it may be added that there are certain anthologies which, while preserving the arrangement in chronological order, yet give only such poems as are suitable for young readers. Such an anthology is the *Lyra Heroica*, edited by the late Mr W. E. Henley.

Another similar collection (which includes within its scope, however, poems other than those purely lyrical) is to be found in the *English Poetry for the Young*, edited by Mr S. E. Winbolt. This latter volume the writer has used with classes of boys of the average age of thirteen or fourteen, and through it has correlated quite effectively the reading of poetry with the teaching of literary history. On the other hand, with a class of pupil-teachers of the average age of seventeen or eighteen the writer has used *The Golden Treasury* as a text-book, taking the poems in the order in which they are given: and the results have been equally satisfactory.

Such are the chief considerations that seem to justify the claim that at a certain stage of the curriculum lyric poetry possesses a distinctive value as a medium for the teaching of English literature; and these considerations determine the particular methods that should be employed in using an anthology in class. In the remainder of this chapter it is proposed to describe briefly a method that may be used in the treatment of individual lyric poems. Since the lessons described deal with individual poems, the general question of correlating the teaching with instruction in literary history will not be considered. As an example of the method applied to the study of a short and simple poem, the unity of which is overlaid by little or no detail, take the case of a lesson dealing with Tennyson's "Bugle Song" in *The Princess*.

The teacher begins by calling upon one or two members of the class to read the poem aloud. He then asks: "What is the subject, the main theme, of this lyric ?" The pupils are required to give particular lines in support of their answers. The main theme, it is concluded, is the effect produced on a lover and his mistress by the echoing sounds of a bugle; the poem may be classed as a love lyric.

"In order that we may understand this more clearly," continues the teacher, "we shall read the poem again." The explanations that have just been given are such as will concentrate the pupils' attention, in this re-reading, upon the essential subject-matter of the poem.

The pupils now proceed, under the teacher's guidance, to trace in detail, verse by verse, the development of the main idea. The poem is written in three verses. The first conveys to us ideas of the place and time that are involved. The imagery of the first part of the verse is expressed in terms of the sense of sight. The last lines sound the main theme of the poem. In the second verse this keynote is further elaborated. Here the imagery is expressed in terms of the sense of hearing. The verse expresses the sound-effects of the echoes as they gradually recede, until at length, coming faintly from afar, they are like thin clear notes blown from fairy bugles. In the third verse the poet passes from the effects produced upon the outer senses, and suggests the more intimate feelings of the two listeners; the echoes faint and die, but always soul will speak to soul.

The poem having been thus read and explained verse by verse, it is re-read as a whole, after which the teacher may ask the pupils to supply such epithets as seem to them to describe appropriately the mood in which it is written—adjectives such as "tender" and "dreamy" and "fanciful" suggest themselves. The attention of the class is then directed to the more formal aspects of the poem. Its movement is light and easy, and the music is characterised by grace and delicacy. Alliteration occurs in "snowy summits," "the long light shakes across the lakes," &c. The metre is chiefly iambic, but there is a variation in the last two lines of each stanza. What is the effect produced by this variation? Are there any imitative sounds in the poem? Show how the formal characteristics that have been mentioned are in harmony with, and aid in the expression of, the main theme and the mood of the lyric.

To illustrate further the application of this method to longer and more complex varieties of lyric poetry, let us now suppose a class to be studying Tennyson's *Ode on the Death of the Duke of Wellington*. Here, as before, the teacher's first object is to secure that the pupils should discover for themselves the main theme. The poem is therefore read as a whole (either at home or in class) and the subject is briefly stated.

The mode in which the general theme is developed through all the particular details has next to be studied. The subject may be said to unfold itself in two main aspects. In the first place, there is a gradual evolution of the theme from the standpoint of "local colour"—the categories of "here" and "now"; there runs throughout the poem a vein of sensuous imagery suggestive of place and time—the thronged streets of London, the booming of the cannon, the wail of the organ, the tears of the crowd, the last rites. In the

second place, there is a gradual evolution of the theme
regarded from a less sensuous and more purely intellectual standpoint; the poet celebrates the Duke's
achievements as a military leader, his high character
as a patriot and a man, and the greatness of his soul.
The poem may be divided structurally into four
sections, each of which marks a development in these
two aspects of its main theme. Stanzas 1 to 4 suggest
to the reader the funeral procession passing through
the crowded streets, and refer in general terms to the
Duke's high character and great deeds. Stanza 5
suggests the arrival of the procession at St Paul's,
"under the cross of gold that shines over city and
river," and introduces the subject of Wellington's
greatness as a soldier. Stanzas 6 to 8 suggest (by
allusion only) the interior of the Cathedral, and
elaborate the previously introduced theme of Wellington's military genius. The last stanza suggests the
closing scene: "ashes to ashes, dust to dust," and
concludes with a reference to a life beyond.

After the first general reading and statement of
the subject-matter, the poem will be re-read in sections
as above, a pause being made at the end of each
section to enable the pupils to trace in it the development of the theme in its two aspects. The attention of
the class will be called specially to certain passages in
which the two threads that run through the poem are
seen to be connected with one another, as to the lines—

> And the volleying cannon thunder his loss.
> He knew their voices of old,

where, by a natural transition, the poet passes from
the present place and time to the celebration of the

Duke's great achievements on the battlefield. Again, in stanza 6, the allusive manner in which the interior of the Cathedral is suggested is worthy of note.

When, by such help as is above indicated, the structure of the *Ode* has taken shape, and its content has been enriched to fulness in the pupils' minds, the poem will then be treated from the formal point of view; and here considerable use may be made of the comparative method. If the " Bugle Song " has been read immediately before the *Ode* the teacher may ask for a comparison between the moods in which the two poems respectively are written. While the mood of the former was characterized as " tender " and " dreamy," that of the latter might be described as " earnest," " exalted," and " spiritual"; and, corresponding with this difference in mood, there are differences in the metrical features of the poems. The metre of the ode is more complex and irregular than that of the song. Its movement is not " light " and " graceful," but " dignified " and " solemn." The frequent recurrence of long vowels, the use of assonance, the repetition of words and phrases will also be noted: and it will be shown how these characteristics are in harmony with the main theme and the mood of the poem; here, as always in the study of poetry, such formal or metrical characteristics will be studied not as being in abstract separation from, but as being vitally connected with, the main subject-matter that is expressed.

CHAPTER VI.

In a subsequent chapter[1] we shall deal briefly with Shakesperean drama as a subject of study for pupils below the age of 14. It will there be pointed out that the method to be followed in junior classes ought to be general, and not detailed, in its application, and should consist mainly in the acting of the plays under suitable conditions. In this chapter we shall be concerned mainly with drama as a subject of study for pupils over 14 or 15. As will be pointed out in Chapter X, while pupils below that age can appreciate and enjoy certain aspects of Shakesperean drama, they cannot appreciate it fully, or essentially as drama. The more serious study of the subject must be held to belong to a later stage of development. This may be demonstrated by a brief consideration of the essential nature of drama and dramatic effect.

The most important element in the drama is the plot or story. This truth was established, in relation to tragedy, as long ago as the time of Aristotle, who, in the *Poetics*, showed how, while the element of character is important in tragedy, it is yet subsidiary to the plot. "Most important of all," he says, "is the structure of the incidents. For Tragedy is an imitation, not of men, but of an action and of life....Dramatic

[1] *v.* Cap. X, pp. 160—163.

action, therefore, is not with a view to the representation of character: character comes in as subsidiary to the action.   Hence the incidents and the plot are the end of a tragedy; and the end is the chief thing of all. Without action there cannot be a tragedy; there may be without character....Again, if you string together a set of speeches expressive of character, and well finished in point of diction and thought, you will not produce the essential tragic effect nearly so well as with a play which, however deficient in these respects, yet has a plot and artistically constructed incidents.... The plot, then, is the first principle, and, as it were, the soul of a tragedy: character holds the second place[1]."   These remarks may be applied with equal force to comedy: true dramatic effect, whether tragical or comical in quality, arises out of the plot and situation.

Tragedy has for its characteristic subject the unsuccessful struggle of man against circumstances: "to be really tragic, it must represent irreparable collision between the individual and the general (in different degrees of generality).   It is the individual with whom we sympathise, and the general of which we recognise the irresistible power[2]."   The character- istic subject of comedy is essentially the same, regarded from an opposite point of view.   While we sympathise with the individual in tragedy, we laugh at him in comedy.   Underlying the collision which ends in

[1] Aristotle's *Poetics*, cap. 6, Mr S. H. Butcher's Translation, 1898.

[2] George Eliot, in her account of the origin and purpose of *The Spanish Gypsy*.

tragedy there may be traced the operation of elemental passions, of dim and incalculable forces beyond the sway of man; underlying the collision which results in comedy there are at work more human and calculable conditions, the pettier emotions and minor follies of man, as vanity or social pride. In some kinds of comedy, however, the more serious side of human nature and the deeper issues of life are also reflected, and this is especially the case in Shakespeare's comedies. No absolute distinction, indeed, can be drawn between the two forms of tragedy and comedy: their real subject is one and the same—each representing an inevitable collision between man and the existing social order.

It is a necessary feature alike of the tragic and the comic plot that this struggle between man and the social order should result in some change of fortune, either from good to bad, or bad to good. Drama must represent human nature in its "traverses of fortune[1]"; and the most typical and effective of dramatic situations, alike in tragedy and in comedy, arises when a character adopts a certain course of action with a particular object in view, and finds that the result which follows is entirely different from what he had intended or anticipated. This is what Aristotle calls περιπέτεια, Reversal or Recoil of the Action, and he includes it as an essential element in a really tragic situation—it must be included as no less essential an element in the situations of comedy. Thus, in the *Electra* of Euripides, Aegisthus goes forth to the plain

---

[1] See Dryden's definition of drama, in his *Essay of Dramatic Poesy*: "Drama is a just and lively image of human nature, in its actions, passions, and traverses of fortune."

to do sacrifice to the Nymphs, intending to secure his
house and person against the enmity of Orestes; and
almost as he prays, Orestes smites him down with the
very sword which had shorn the peace-offering.   In
Hamlet, again, the king and Laertes poison the foil, so
that Hamlet may be killed in the fencing-match; and
they are themselves slain by the poisoned weapon.
In *Twelfth Night*, Malvolio assumes the part of a lover,
and is locked up as a madman; Sir Andrew Aguecheek
boldly attacks Sebastian, judging him (from the
previous behaviour of his " double " Viola) to be a
coward, and emerges from the struggle himself dis-
graced. Alike in tragedy and in comedy, life is repre
sented as a game of cross-purposes: the calculations of
men are astray, and the results they achieve do not
correspond with their expectations. The contrariness of
life is reflected in the " irony " of the dramatist in a
twofold manner—in the first place, when the actions that
he depicts are followed by a result different from what
had been intended by the actors, and again when the
speeches that he puts into the mouths of his characters
convey a truth unsuspected by the speakers.   Examples
of this irony underlying speech are numerous both
in tragedy and in comedy.   When Othello meets
Desdemona in Cyprus, he exclaims, " If it were now to
die, 'twere now to be most happy"—not recognising,
in his ignorance of the future, the fulness of truth
contained in his words.   In *Richard II* the king, when
opposed by Bolingbroke, expresses, in high-sounding
phrases, his entire confidence in the success of his
enterprise, while all the time the audience knows that
the Welsh army on which his hopes rest has dispersed.

In *As You Like It* and *Twelfth Night* the humour of
the scenes in which the disguised Rosalind and Viola
appear is greatly heightened by the fact that, while
the audience knows that they are girls, the characters
on the stage believe them to be boys. The effect of
dramatic irony, in all its manifestations, depends on a
sense of contrast and surprise in the minds of the
audience: when the circumstances are tragic, the sense
of contrast is accompanied by pity or terror; when
comic, the audience is moved to mirth. Drama aims
at presenting a lively image of life itself; and as life
plays with the ignorance of man, and is full of strange
surprises and piquant or bitter contrasts, so is it too in
drama. Along with the "Reversal of the Action"
Aristotle includes what he calls $\dot{a}\nu a\gamma\nu\dot{\omega}\rho\iota\sigma\iota\varsigma$ ("Recognition") as an essential part of the Tragic Plot, and he
defines this as "a change from ignorance to knowledge,
producing love or hate between the persons destined
by the poet for good or bad fortune[1]." Understood in
a broad sense, and as being at bottom forms of
dramatic irony, depending upon surprises, both $\pi\epsilon\rho\iota$-
$\pi\dot{\epsilon}\tau\epsilon\iota a$ and $\dot{a}\nu a\gamma\nu\dot{\omega}\rho\iota\sigma\iota\varsigma$ are essential elements alike of
the Tragic and the Comic Plot.

An analysis of the nature of dramatic plot indicates
to the teacher that the more serious study of drama,
as drama, presupposes a somewhat advanced stage
of mental development on the part of the pupil. In
drama human action is regarded from a particular point
of view which cannot be adequately grasped by the
young. The compelling force of circumstances and the
established social order, the subtler and deeper contrasts

---

[1] *Poetics*, XI. 2.

and surprises of reality, with which drama deals, cannot
be rightly understood by them. Action is regarded and
represented by the dramatist as being essentially conditioned by a mode of thought or feeling, and the con-
ditioning mental states that underlie action in drama
are frequently of a subtle or complicated kind. In the
plot of fiction, on the other hand, the actions depicted
need not necessarily be so conditioned : an effective and
stirring romance may tell a tale of vigorous and gallant
action into which the deeper and more refined phases
of thought and feeling do not enter, and again, a novel
may aim rather at the delineation of character or the
exposition of dialogue than at the representation of
action. The very limitations of stage-representation
impose a corresponding limitation on the nature of
the actions that are suitable for dramatic treatment.
For instance, great material movements, or actions pre-
supposing the presence of a large number of persons,
cannot be adequately represented on the stage. Drury
Lane melodrama may attempt, indeed, to reproduce a
scene at a racecourse or the wreck of a great liner;
but the resources even of Drury Lane are not sufficient
to make these reproductions dramatically impressive.
In true drama, actions are regarded by the dramatist
not from a purely objective standpoint, in and for
themselves, or merely as spectacle, but in their relation
to the mental states which condition or are conditioned
by them. The murders in Greek tragedy are enacted
off the stage ; but the dramatist represents vividly the
states of mind and the crises of thought and feeling
which lead up to them. Shakespeare's dramatic power
is shown in the representation not of such a material

act as the murder of Desdemona, but of the mental agonies of Othello. Action in drama is thus much more deeply based on thought than is the case generally in fiction, and this circumstance indicates to the teacher that the study of drama as drama cannot effectively be begun before the age of 15 or 16. A play may be read by junior pupils for certain qualities that are not intrinsically dramatic—for its presentment of an interesting story, for its detached incidents, for the broad delineation of character, or for the poetic beauty of detached passages, but its essentially dramatic qualities cannot be rightly appreciated.

Again, the division of drama into scenes and acts makes it difficult to grasp the structure as a continuous whole. Yet it is essential that a pupil should be affected with this sense of unity and completeness in studying a play. The structure may be simple or complex : that is, it may be built along a single thread of interest, or with the main thread of the plot it may follow other minor threads; but in either case an essential feature of a well-constructed play is that it should affect the hearer or reader with a sense of unity : every scene in a good play may be said to serve a definite purpose, as contributing to unity of impression. When the structure is complex, the different threads of the plot, while apparently diverting attention from the main theme, are connected with it in such a manner that really they emphasize its importance and interpret its meaning. An instance of this is found in the frequently occurring dramatic " fugue," in which an important situation in the main plot is reproduced, with variations, in an underplot. Thus, in *Hamlet*, the

6—2

situation of Laertes, when he acts under the sense of a
wrong done to his sister, corresponds with the situation
of Hamlet, whose father has been wronged, and Hamlet's
character is interpreted for us by the contrast between
his and Laertes' behaviour in similar circumstances.
Again, in *The Merchant of Venice*, Bassanio's wooing is
paralleled by Gratiano's : both win their brides at the
same time, both receive rings, and both give them away.
Frequently, too, the threads in a complex plot are
woven with a view, not to resemblance, but to contrast :
for example, in *Twelfth Night*, side by side with the
romance of the more serious plot, there runs the humorous byplay of the underplot. Always, however, in a
well-constructed play, the threads of the plot are invented
in such a manner as will contribute to the essential
unity of impression that should be produced. The
teacher's main object in the study of structure should
be, negatively, to overcome and eradicate the disparted
impression which the division into scenes and acts is
apt to convey, and, positively, to impress the pupil
with a sense of unity. With a view to the attainment
of this object, after the first reading of a play, the
pupils may be required to state briefly in writing the
purpose or purposes of each scene in relation to one
another and to the whole.

Closely connected with the study of the plot is the
study of the characters. In drama generally, and in
the great tragedies particularly, story and character are
adapted to one another. The *Medea* of Euripides tells
how a woman has been forsaken by her lover, who
seeks to marry another; and the characters of the
actors make the tragic collision of the drama inevit-

able. All Shakespeare's tragedies show an unerring harmony between story and character. In certain kinds of comedy, however,—as the comedy of intrigue —this correspondence is not so absolute: here the claims of the story are considered almost exclusively: the dramatist's sole preoccupation seems to be to secure that the movement and interest of the story should be sustained, and the characters are frequently made to act not consistently or probably, so as to produce the impression of real life, but merely in such a manner as will help towards the working out of the plot. Thus, in *Twelfth Night*, Orsino protests a changeless love for Olivia, but quite suddenly, and without apparent reason, transfers his affections to Viola. In the reading of plays like *Hamlet* or *Othello* a detailed consideration of the chief characters is necessary to the understanding of the story. In the reading of plays like *Twelfth Night*, on the other hand, where the character-drawing is for the most part not elaborate or carefully studied, it would be absurd to attempt to analyze the characters with great minuteness: most of them are merely pieces on a board, to be used in working out the convenient solution in a particular game of comedy. In the study of character the teacher should always be guided by the relation of the characters to the main theme and central interest: the *dramatis personae* should not be studied as independent entities; and, in the case of dramas in which story and character are not adapted to one another, the study of character should not be forced. The following passage from Professor Raleigh's monograph on *Shakespeare* expresses admirably the point of view from which character in drama should be considered. " The critics," he says, "must needs be wiser than Shakespeare, and must finish his sketches for him, telling us more about his characters than ever he knew....They alter the focus, and force all things to illustrate this detail or that. They plead reverence for Shakespeare's omniscience, and pay a very poor compliment to his art. A play is like a piano; if it is tuned to one key, it is out of tune for every other. The popular saying which denies all significance to the play of *Hamlet* with the Prince of Denmark left out, shows a just sense of this. Yet the study of the lesser characters, conceived in relation, not to Hamlet, but to one another, continues to exercise the critics. The King in *Hamlet* is little better than a man of straw. He is sufficiently realized for Shakespeare's purpose; we see him through Hamlet's eyes, and share Hamlet's hatred of him....The analysis and illustration of Shakespeare's characters, considered separately, has had so long a vogue, and has produced work so memorable, that we are in some danger of forgetting how partial such a method must be....We are lured further and further afield, until we find ourselves arguing on questions that have no meaning for criticism, and no existence save in dreams. It is well to go back to Shakespeare; and to remember the conditions imposed upon him, whether by the story of his choice, or by the necessities of dramatic presentment[1]."

In the study of drama generally, the most important objects of consideration are plot, structure,

[1] *Shakespeare.* By Walter Raleigh. London: Macmillan & Co., 1907. Pages 153—6.

and character, each of which should be regarded as combining to produce a particular dramatic effect. The diction and style of play, however, must also receive consideration; and in the case of Shakespeare's plays, when older pupils are concerned, this part of the work may be made to produce especially valuable results. From a philological point of view, the history of our vocabulary and grammar is illustrated; and from a more purely literary point of view, the richness and flexibility of the English language, and its power of expressing the subtler shades of meaning, are nowhere so conspicuously shown as in Shakespeare's plays. In them, too, our pupils may study the nature of blank verse and its variations as a medium for dramatic and poetic expression. The consideration of the sources of the plots, and their treatment by Shakespeare, furnishes a suitable introduction to an aspect of literary study which should be included in any complete curriculum; and the consideration of Shakesperean criticism and bibliography may be made to form an introduction to the principles of criticism and bibliography generally. All these branches of Shakesperean study should of course be undertaken only in the senior classes, with pupils of the age of 17 or 18, and they should not be regarded as objects of study for their own sake exclusively, but rather as adding to our conception of the artistic qualities and greatness of the plays. Finally, the study of Shakespeare should also be comparative: our pupils should compare particular plays or groups of plays, and trace the growth of his mind and art.

Nor should the dramatic study of our pupils be confined to Shakespeare. At a later stage there should

certainly be included in the course the study, in a good
English translation, of one or more of the great Greek
tragedies. No other dramas are so well fitted to impress
the reader or hearer with a right sense of dramatic
effect. The Greek tragic writers were restricted in their
themes to certain current legends, but their subjects
were characteristically tragic. And again, many of the
artistic laws which Aeschylus, Sophocles, and Euripides
observed are not arbitrary and of limited application,
but essential to the nature of true drama generally.
Greek tragedy is marked by simplicity of plot, severity
of structure, and adaptation of story and character : in
it the unity of impression which drama should convey
is not blurred by the presentation of subsidiary details,
and we are enabled the more easily to perceive the
dramatic point of the story. As a means whereby our
pupils may appreciate better the qualities of Shakesperean drama, no more effective plan could be devised
than the successive reading of a Greek and of a Shakesperean tragedy. Euripides's *Electra* and Shakespeare's
Hamlet suggest themselves as suitable plays for this
purpose. The two plays resemble one another in subject,
but differ widely in treatment. In the *Electra* the
unities of time and place are observed, and there is also
unity of impression ; in *Hamlet* the unities of time and
place are broken, but the essential unity of impression
is preserved amid all the diversity of the plot and tone
and characterization. A wider reading and comparison
of Greek and Shakesperean drama should help our
pupils to realize more vividly the imperial scope of
Shakespeare's genius : his sympathy with and zest for
life in all its aspects, grave and gay, and his infinitely
varied power of dramatic presentment.

CHAPTER VII.

AN essential characteristic of true narrative poetry is that it treats its subjects objectively and impersonally. The writer in this kind surrenders, as it were, the consciousness of his own individuality, and aims at representing impersonally the actions and feelings of others. In this respect he differs from the lyric poet, whose poems are more intimately expressive of his own personality.

The simplest form of narrative poetry is the ballad, or short story in verse, and within this form two kinds may be distinguished: the traditional or authentic, and the modern or literary.

The traditional ballads were sung or recited by minstrels, and their original authors are unknown. The chief subjects of which they treat are feats of arms, perilous and strange adventures by sea or land, magic spells, love and romance. They reflect the more elemental feelings and facts of life: hatred and love, courage, treachery, vengeance, fear, the struggle of man with man and with mysterious alien powers. In many of them there is a strongly marked supernatural element. The plots and contrivances of fairies and supernatural beings, who are nearly always hostile to men, the working of magic spells, the transformations of human beings into birds and animals, the sending of messages and the communication of secrets by birds, the reappearance of the dead—such are some of the magical and super-natural effects that commonly occur in the ballad narratives. Some of them, again, as, for instance, *King John and the Abbot of Canterbury*, in which the story, like many old stories, turns upon the answer to a riddle, are humorous in tone. Others, like *Chevy Chase*, the *Robin Hood* ballads, and *Sir Patrick Spens*, have a historical background; while others, such as *King Lear*, *King Cophetua*, and *The Jew of Venice*, are interesting because of their literary associations. The style of the traditional ballad is marked by naivete, sometimes by a certain crudeness, and by brevity, simplicity, direct-ness, dramatic power, energy, and freshness of feeling.

The imitative modern ballads resemble the tradi-tional in subject-matter and style; they, too, are short stories in verse, told simply and vividly. Some of them, such as *The Wild Huntsman, The Wreck of the Hesperus*, and *Lord Ullin's Daughter*, keep close to the style of the traditional ballad; while others, like Tennyson's *The Revenge*, are more elaborate in their treatment and more finished in style. In general, they do not possess the rugged strength and freshness of feeling of the old ballads, though many of them are marked by charac-teristic excellences of their own.

The qualities of the ballad, in both subject-matter and style, make it especially suitable reading for junior pupils. Examples illustrative of its various typical themes should be read, and when questioning is used it should be made a means of impressing on the pupils the general character of the subject-matter, as dealing with war and combat, or adventure, love, magic, etc., and as being pathetic, or humorous, or tragic, or romantic, etc., in tone. The main features of the language and style and metre may also be noted if the teacher wishes. Many of the more exquisite ballads, however, should never be analysed with any detail, nor used for language exercises: these may be read aloud expressively, and commented upon briefly, by the teacher, and afterwards, if time should permit, learned by heart by the pupils. The historical background and literary associations of some of the ballads should be made clear. If a collection is used, it is advisable that it should contain examples of the imitative as well as of the authentic ballads. The comparative method will often be found useful. For instance, if a class had read *Sir Patrick Spens*, and was afterwards reading *The Wreck of the Hesperus*, the pupils might be asked to state how they resemble one another in subject-matter. Both contain a vivid description of a storm and shipwreck. In both, too, the element of superstition is introduced under similar circumstances. In the old ballad, when Sir Patrick orders his men to "make ready," one of the sailors protests:

> Now, ever alack! my master dear,
>   I fear a deadly storm.
> I saw the new moon, late yestreen,
>   Wi' the auld moon in her arm,
> And if we gang to sea, master,
>   I fear we'll come to harm.

In Longfellow's poem a similar passage occurs:

> Then up and spake an old sailor,
>   Had sailed the Spanish Main:
> "I pray thee put into yonder port,
>   For I fear a hurricane.

> Last night the moon had a golden ring,
>   And to-night no moon we see."
> The skipper he blew a whiff from his pipe,
>   And a scornful laugh laughed he.

The main characteristics of the ballad-form, both as regards subject-matter and treatment, may be most conveniently impressed on the pupils by the method of comparison, in the course of the successive reading of different ballads.

We shall now illustrate the preceding remarks with more detailed reference to *The Ancient Ballad of Chevy Chase*.

In dealing with this ballad, after a brief reference to Border life and Border feuds in the middle ages, the teacher might first read the whole poem aloud.

The subject-matter might then be discussed. The pupils should reproduce the story simply in their own words. What passages are especially notable for the expression of chivalrous feeling? The following might be quoted and read aloud by the pupils: lls. 73–98 (Douglas's proposal to settle the quarrel by single combat, Percy's acceptance, and Wytharynton's refusal to acquiesce in this arrangement); lls. 123–130 (Douglas's proposal for a truce, and Percy's refusal to yield); lls. 141–148 (Percy's panegyric on the dead Douglas). What lines or passages are remarkable for vivid description? Such lines as "Bowmen bicker'd upon the bent" (l. 21), "greyhounds thorough the grevés glent" (l. 25), "his armour glittered as a glede" (l. 57), "they swapt together till they both swet" (l. 113), might be quoted, and comment might be made on their chief features— the use of alliteration, the expressiveness of the verbs denoting action, the simile, etc. What lines illustrate

well the poet's power of imagining details? Some of
the more sanguinary details are instanced with extra-
ordinary vividness and gusto, as when Douglas and
Percy are described as fighting

> Till the blood out of their basnets sprent
> As ever did hail or rain;

or in the lines describing the "dint" with which Sir
Hugh the Montgomery slew the Lord Percy:

> With a surè spear of a mighty tree
> Through the body him he bore,
> *O' the t'other side that a man might see*
> *A large cloth-yard and more*;

or when Montgomery's own death at the hand of the
Northumbrian archer is narrated:

> An archer of Northumberland
>   Saw slain was the Lord Percy;
> He bare a bent-bow in his hand
>   Was made of a trusty tree.
> An arrow that was a cloth-yard long
>   To the hard steel halèd he;
> A dint that was both sad and sore
>   He set on Montgomery.
> The dint it was both sad and sair
>   That he on Montgomery set;
> *The swan-feathers that his arrow bare*
> *With his heart-blood they were wet.*

The pupils' conception of the subject-matter having
been thus enlarged and enriched, the question might be
asked: In what style should such a ballad be read or
recited? and they might then be called upon to read
aloud, the poem being subdivided for this purpose into
a number of parts each dealing, as far as possible, with
a single incident or phase. In the course of this reading

the meanings of some of the old or obsolete words might be explained, and further comment made, if desired, on the language and style. The directness and dramatic quality of the narrative, as shown in the use of dialogue, which is a characteristic feature of many of the ballads, might be noticed, with such features as the frequent use of monosyllabic words, the repetition of words and lines, the fixed epithet in "doughty Douglas," the repetition of particular consonant-sounds, etc. This detailed treatment, however, should not be overdone, and should be subsidiary and related as closely as possible to the expressive reading of the ballad.

In conclusion, some of the best readers in the class might be called upon to read the whole poem without interruption, and then, if the teacher wished, he might discuss briefly the historical basis of the ballad, taking the opportunity of pointing out the vagueness and inaccuracy of the history it contains, in which respect it is characteristic of ballad literature generally.

Akin to the ballad, and resembling it in some respects, though far different in others, is the epic. Like the ballad, epic poetry comprises two kinds: the authentic or traditional, sometimes called the "epic of growth," of which *Beowulf* and the *Iliad* or *Odyssey* may be taken as examples, and the imitative or literary or classical, such as Vergil's *Æneid* and Milton's *Paradise Lost*. Both kinds deal with the deeds of heroes, generally the legendary heroes of a race, and in both mythology and supernaturalism play a prominent part. They differ, however, in that the authentic epic is of a simpler and more naive character, and deals with legends that were still alive in the hearts of the poet's original audience, while in the classical epic the style conforms more or less to an established convention, and the legendary basis of the story is derived from the poet's reading and literary research.

The main characteristics of the epic as a literary form are well indicated in the following passages from Professor Macneile Dixon's *English Epic and Heroic Poetry*[1]:

" The true epic, wherever created, will be a narrative poem, organic in structure, dealing with great actions and great characters, in a style commensurate with the lordliness of its theme, which tends to idealise its characters, and to sustain and embellish its subject by means of episode and amplification....

" While conciseness, rapidity, intensity belong to the soul of drama, the epic, diffuse, leisurely, spacious, of necessity unfolds its action with circumlocution; what it yields to drama—and it must yield in depth and heat of emotion—it attempts to recover from it in extent of picturesque and engaging surface. Tragedy is a rapid mountain torrent plunging through dark valley and gloomy ravine; epic a broad and equable stream moving with unhurrying and level sweep through the broad and shining plain....

" Great epic owes much of its dignity to the mere spaciousness of its action, its majestic proportions....Its interest, like that of drama, is dependent upon action and character, upon the story and the persons. These two, upon either of which it might be imprudent to lay the major stress, are the pillars of epic. Further, the

[1] *English Epic and Heroic Poetry.* By W. Macneile Dixon, M.A. London : J. M. Dent and Sons, Ltd. 1912.

action must be great or important action, and the characters great or important characters. Of themselves great actions and great characters impart that dignity, the uplifting strain, without which the poem lays no claim to epic honours, a certain elevation of tone, proper to the theme and to the conduct of the theme."

So far as English literature is concerned, the study of epic poetry in schools practically means the study of *Paradise Lost*. *Paradise Regained* is seldom read, and its poetic achievement cannot be compared with that of *Paradise Lost*; while the study of *Beowulf* belongs properly to the University stage. There are many reasons why *Paradise Lost* should be included as an essential part of the literature course in Secondary and Continuation Schools. In the first place, of course, it should be read for its intrinsic qualities as great poetry, and as a means of enabling our pupils to study the epic form. A further reason for its inclusion in the curriculum is that those who do not acquire some knowledge of *Paradise Lost* at school are not so likely to read it on their own initiative in later life; for the tendencies of to-day, it must be admitted, are not favourable either to the writing or the reading of long poems conceived on the scale and in the manner of *Paradise Lost*. Yet who that had not read Milton's masterpiece could be said to possess any adequate knowledge of English literature or of the power and scope of the English language as a medium for imaginative expression?

The characteristics of the poem, alike in subject-matter, form, and style, indicate that it should not be studied until the age of 15 or 16 has been reached. In particular, the wealth of its historical and literary allusions, the vastness of the learning it displays, makes it unsuitable reading for junior pupils.

From this feature, too, the inference may be drawn that the method appropriate to the treatment of the poem in class should be somewhat detailed. The greatness of *Paradise Lost* as poetry does not, indeed, depend upon its learning; but much of it must be more or less unintelligible to the reader that does not possess some knowledge of the historical and literary allusions.

At the same time, its treatment should also be general, in this sense, that the detailed study of particular passages should be accompanied by the more general and rapid reading of a considerable part, if not the whole, of the poem. In most classes the time available will probably not permit of the whole poem being read, but at least Books I to IV should be taken. The study of, say, a single Book can give no adequate idea of the epic form in general, or of the characteristic qualities of *Paradise Lost* in particular. An essential feature of the epic is the largeness of its scope, which appears not only in the sublimity of its characters, or in its imaginative greatness, or in the grandeur of its style, but also, outwardly, in its mere length. As we read further into *Paradise Lost,* our conception of Milton's greatness as a poet, and our taste for his poetry, inevitably grow.

When only a part of the poem is read, the pupils should study the "arguments" prefixed to each of the twelve Books, so that they may form some idea of the structure of the poem as a whole.

Most of the pupils' reading may be done as "homework," but, as has been remarked above, a considerable amount of detailed study and discussion and reading aloud in class will also be necessary. The style of the poem, dignified, sustained, and often rhetorical, makes it particularly suitable for reading aloud.

The passages chosen for detailed study may be those the teacher thinks most beautiful, or those that illustrate clearly Milton's characteristic excellences— the stateliness and sublimity of his imagination, the sustained grandeur of his style, the majestic music of his verse, the infinitely skilful sequence of "verse-paragraphs," with "the sense variously drawn out from one verse into another," the harmony of sound with sense.

Other passages may be selected to illustrate Milton's learning. References to classical literature, and to the legendary lore of ancient Greece and Rome, occur on almost every page of *Paradise Lost*, and classical influence accounts for many features of the style and structure also (*cf.*, *e.g.*, the Homeric similes, and, in Book I, the invocation of the Muse at the beginning, and the list of the fallen gods in lls. 376–521—a counterpart, as Addison points out, to Homer's catalogue of the ships and Vergil's list of warriors). The influence of the Bible appears not only in the general conception and spirit of the poem, but in hundreds of verbal allusions. Many passages, again, show the influence of English and Italian literature, and, in particular, as Mr Courthope remarks in his *History of English Poetry*, "the imagery of the romances...furnished [Milton] with frequent similes and allusions for the illustration of his angelic action[1]" (*cf.*, *e.g.*, Book I, lls. 581–587, 763–766).

[1] *A History of English Poetry*. By W. J. Courthope, C.B. Vol. III. p. 414. Macmillan and Co., Ltd. 1903.

A knowledge of the varied literary influences that pervade Milton's work will add to our pupils' appreciation of the greatness of his achievement.

Another kind of narrative poetry is the metrical romance, and with it we may include what may be described generally as romantic narrative poetry. In this kind Spenser's *Faerie Queene* should be read: its stories of chivalrous adventure, love, and magic, when told in prose form, will attract the youngest; but the poem itself, in its original form, may more suitably be studied by senior pupils. The works of Coleridge, Southey, Byron, Tennyson, Arnold, William Morris, etc., will provide other examples of romantic narrative poetry. But, of all the poems of this class that our literature contains, those of Walter Scott may be considered to be the best adapted for general use in schools.

The characteristic qualities that attract young readers to Scott's poetry are, mainly, the characteristic qualities of the old ballads and romances. It tells a story simply and vividly, is full of movement, and depicts in clear and bright colours the pictorial aspects of life in times when these were more conspicuous than they are in the life of to-day. Above all, there is in it nothing of the subjectivity that is so marked a feature of later poetry. In this respect a striking contrast may be drawn between Scott's poems and, for instance, such a narrative poem as *The Idylls of the King*, in which the writer is not interested primarily in the actions of his characters but in their ideas, and an allegorical purpose underlies the whole narrative. If we read, for example, *The Lay of the Last Minstrel*, and, immediately afterwards, one of the *Idylls*—say *The Passing of Arthur*, we see at once

7—2

how, while Scott tells his story objectively, and with a sheer delight in action in and for itself, Tennyson is more interested in describing his hero's mental states. The fight with Modred, for instance, is only briefly indicated, but the description of Arthur's meditations is worked out with much detail and great psychological insight. Of all the modern poets, Scott displays most clearly and fully the qualities of the epic spirit, which is essentially objective in character. His poetry is lacking, indeed, in sustained dignity and elevation of style, and in that respect falls short of epic rank; but in both its subject-matter and its treatment it approximates more nearly to the epic than does any other modern poetry. If, then, we wish our pupils to study narrative poetry in its purer forms, untouched by the spirit of introspection, and carrying on the tradition of the old ballads and metrical romances, and of Homer and the authentic epic, we must turn their attention to the poetry of Scott rather than that of any other modern writer.

Some suggestions may now be made as to the method in which Scott's longer poems may be treated in class. The following remarks refer particularly to *The Lay of the Last Minstrel*, but the principles they embody may be applied more generally to Scott's other poems also.

Before the actual reading begins, the teacher may say a few words on the historical basis of the story, indicating the approximate date of the action and referring to the feud between the Scotts and the Kerrs; so that the class may be prepared, when they read the first Canto, to understand at once the difficulty that confronts the two lovers, Margaret of Branksome and Lord Cranstoun.

The reading of the poem may be done in class, mostly by the pupils themselves. The subject-matter is simple, and the style clear, therefore the pupils should be able to read fairly well even at the first attempt. The teacher, too, should take some part in the reading. With a view to maintaining the pupils' interest, it may be advisable that, until the first reading has been completed, the books should be retained by the teacher and given out to the class each time they are to be used; under the circumstances, it is in some respects not desirable that the pupils should have read the poem previously at home.

The reading should proceed with as few interruptions as possible, so that the atmosphere of the poem may be preserved. Even the calling of individual pupils by name to read should be avoided. Each pupil in succession may read one or a stated number of stanzas; or the Cantos may be divided into short sections of varying length, each dealing with its own theme and assigned beforehand to a particular pupil for reading: the class should understand clearly that, as soon as one member has finished reading, his or her successor should continue without waiting to be called upon.

At the end of each Canto the subject-matter may be discussed. In this discussion the teacher will find it helpful to remember that, in its preoccupation with war, romantic love, and supernatural belief, the poem reflects three important aspects of the old ballads and romances. We may distinguish three threads in the story, dealing respectively with: (1) the feud between the Scotts and the Kerrs; (2) the love affair of Margaret of Branksome and Lord Cranstoun; (3) the episode of Gilpin Horner. After each Canto has been read, the pupils may be asked to indicate the stanzas that deal more exclusively with those themes. Thus, in Canto I, stanzas 1–8 relate mainly to the feud between the Scotts and the Kerrs, stanzas 9–18 to the love affair of Margaret and Lord Cranstoun, and stanzas 19–31 to the episode of Gilpin Horner. But each thread of the plot is interwoven with the others. The romantic and the supernatural aspects of the tale must be considered to be less important than the warlike: the real interest of the poem does not lie in the love-story, nor in the episode of the Goblin Page, but in the vivid picture it gives of Border life, and, accordingly, it is this aspect that the teacher should seek to impress most vividly upon the pupils.

When all the Cantos have been read, the structure of the poem as a whole may be reviewed. Its chief weakness is that the supernatural episode of Gilpin Horner does not really form an integral and organic part of the plot, although it is connected with it at certain points. But it should be remembered, too, that this episode helps considerably to create the characteristic atmosphere of the poem and is quite in line with the traditions of the old metrical romance. The question will naturally arise: Is Canto VI superfluous? Structurally considered, it is seen to be connected but loosely with the rest of the poem, the only purpose it serves being that it enables the poet to dispose of Gilpin Horner. On other grounds, however, the Canto could not well be spared: its tone harmonises perfectly with the rest of the poem, and it contains some beautiful passages, including the ballad of "Rosabelle" and the famous lines beginning "Breathes there a man with soul so dead." The setting of the poem as the lay of the last minstrel should be noted, and also the minstrel's occasional digressions suggested by points in the narrative—these are in keeping with the traditional epic manner of garrulity and digression.

The subject-matter and structure having been considered, the poem, or, if the time available should be limited, selected portions of it, may be read again and studied with more detail. In the course of this second reading the chief characteristics of the language, style, and versification should be treated, and, in particular, the use of old and obsolete words, the energy of the style, Scott's characteristic method of description by colour, and the skill with which he varies the metre according to the sense, should be illustrated.

A fourth variety of narrative poetry is realistic in its tendency and depicts the world of our everyday experience. This type has lately become popular in the works of Masefield and other writers. Poems such as Goldsmith's *Deserted Village*, Longfellow's *Evangeline*, and Tennyson's *Enoch Arden* belong to it, and are suitable for study in class.

The method that may be adopted by the teacher in the treatment of this kind is similar to the method that has just been described, and there is no need to elaborate it further. All that need be said is that, in the case of every poem set for class-study, the teacher should have previously formed an adequate conception of its subject-matter, structure, style, and atmosphere, and the precise methods he will follow in his teaching will be determined in accordance with that conception.

CHAPTER VIII.

THE STUDY OF SPEECHES.

THE oration as a form of expression is marked by distinctive characteristics that impart to the study of it a special interest and enable us to deal in the English curriculum with subject-matter that cannot be so conveniently treated through any other form.

One of its advantages is that we may use it to illustrate the principles of effective discourse—to show, for instance, that a discourse, if it is to achieve its purpose, if it is to produce conviction, must be well arranged, the successive propositions being logically sequent and coherent and the arguments so grouped and welded together as to produce a cumulative effect. Again, from the examination of particular instances, it may be shown that the arrangement of arguments is of special importance at the beginning and the end of a discourse, those being critical points, at which a speaker or writer should make an effort to attack strongly and possess wholly the minds of those whom he is addressing. Another question that our pupils may be led to consider in relation to the arrangement of arguments is: at what point in a discourse is it best to deal with the arguments of an opponent? It will be found that, as a general rule, the refutation of opposed arguments is best placed in the middle of a speech; but it occurs also frequently at the beginning and the end[1].

Another advantage to be gained from a study of the speech-form is that we may use it to introduce our pupils informally to the study of rhetorical logic or logic applied to ordinary argument. Everyone will agree as to the utility of teaching boys and girls while yet at school to appreciate the value of evidence in argument and to distinguish accurately between sound and fallacious reasoning, and it is by the consideration of concrete arguments actually used by speakers that such teaching can be given most effectively. The study of logical principles taught in this way will be seen to be in close touch with the needs of our daily lives. In the reading of a single oration the various methods of argument used by speakers may be explained, and their validity, with the conditions on which it depends, may be examined, and opportunities will be afforded of discussing the fallacies and weaknesses that most commonly occur in argument[2].

Suppose, for example, that the following passage had been read in class:

"Perhaps there are in this room—I am sure there are in the country—many persons who hold a superstitious traditionary belief that, somehow or other, our vast trade is to be attributed to what we have done in this way, that it is thus we have opened markets

---

[1] For a discussion of the arrangement of arguments in a speech the reader may be referred to a little book by the present writer, entitled *How to Argue Successfully : a Study of the Principles and Methods of Argument* (Geo. Routledge and Sons, Ltd.), v. Cap. VIII.

[2] For a detailed account of the various kinds of argument employed in discourse v. op. cit., *How to Argue Successfully*.

and advanced commerce, that English greatness depends upon the extent of English conquests and English military renown. But I am inclined to think that, with the exception of Australia, there is not a single dependency of the Crown which, if we come to reckon what it has cost in war and protection, would not be found to be a positive loss to the people of this country. Take the United States, with which we have such an enormous and constantly increasing trade. The wise statesmen of the last generation, men whom your school histories tell you were statesmen, serving under a monarch who they tell you was a patriotic monarch, spent £130,000,000 of the fruits of the industry of the people in a vain—happily a vain—endeavour to retain the colonies of the United States in subjection to the monarchy of England. Add up the interest of that £130,000,000 for all this time, and how long do you think it will be before there will be a profit on the trade with the United States which will repay the enormous sum we invested in a war to retain those states as colonies of this Empire? It never will be paid off. Wherever you turn, you will find that the opening of markets, developing of new countries, introducing cotton cloth with cannon balls, are vain, foolish, and wretched excuses for wars, and ought not to be listened to for a moment by any man who understands the multiplication table, or who can do the simplest sum in arithmetic[1]."

After the reading of this passage the pupils might be asked to state briefly in their own words, and to classify, the argument that it propounds, and to point out any weakness or flaw in the argument. The con-

[1] John Bright, at Birmingham, October 29, 1858.

clusion sought to be established is that English wars
and conquests, so far from increasing, have actually
diminished our national wealth and greatness; and to
establish this proposition the speaker cites the War
of American Independence as a case in point. We have
here an induction from example; and it may be criti-
cised as affording an instance of " hasty generalisation."
Only one case is cited—that of the American War—
and the speaker s opponents might argue that this was
an exceptional, and not a typical, case, since our defeat
by the American colonists involved the loss of our
American possessions.

The following exercises may serve to illustrate
further how the study of speeches may be used to
develop in our pupils a faculty of logical discrimination.
The work may be done either orally, by discussion with
and among the pupils, or, after a certain amount of
oral practice has been given, in written form:

(1) Comment on the logical value of the following
retort made by Mr Gladstone to a charge of obstruction
brought against his party:

"I myself charged the Tory opposition under the
late Government with obstruction. I will give you a
specimen. We proposed a plan of Closure of Debate....
That proposal, which was so feeble that it never but
once was brought into operation, and then it was not
worth putting into operation—that proposal, on the
pretext of respect for liberty of debate, was opposed by
the Tory party for nineteen nights altogether. There
is obstruction! There are the masters of it! There are
the professors of it!"

The fallacy of *ignoratio elenchi*, "ignoring of the

question," may be said to be here involved, in the form
of an *argumentum ad hominem* or *tu quoque* argument.

(2) " An attack has recently been made upon the
Throne on account of the costliness of the institution "
(Lord Beaconsfield).—Classify and give a short account
of the argument used by Lord Beaconsfield to refute this
attack. Can the argument from analogy, used by itself,
ever be really conclusive ? Give reasons for your answer.

(3) " Considering that you [Mr Gladstone] stated in
1886 that the wit of man could not devise a plan for
retaining the Irish representation at Westminster,
how is it that you say now that there are a great many
modes in which it can be done ? "—Does this prove Mr
Gladstone to have been wrong in his second opinion ?
What, from a strictly logical point of view, is the value
of a charge of inconsistency against an opponent, even
if the charge be substantiated ? What fallacy is involved ?

(4) Examine the validity of the following, considered
as an argument in favour of Free Trade :

" For upwards of half a century Free Trade has
been the mainspring and source of our national prosperity. To the abolition of protective duties is due the
vast increase of our wealth in recent years. For many
years before the adoption of Free Trade our commerce
was almost at a standstill."

It may be objected that in this argument the speaker
has selected only one out of several or many operative
conditions, and has described it as being the sole cause
of our national prosperity. Such essential factors in
the increase of wealth as the development of railways
and improvements in machinery are ignored.

(5) "If one-twentieth part of what has been said is true, if I am entitled to any measure of your approbation, I may begin to think that my public career and my opinions are not so un-English and so anti-national as some of those who profess to be the best of our public instructors have sometimes assumed" (John Bright).—Is it a good argument against any opinion or proposal to say that it is "un-English"? Give reasons for your answer.

In many of the arguments that we read daily in books and newspapers, or use ourselves in discussion, fallacies are frequently found, and the inductive method is often applied in an excessively loose fashion, with a much less degree of strictness than that of which the subject may admit. Teaching that will train the senior pupils in Secondary and Continuation Schools to detect the weakness and insufficiency of such arguments ought to be of much practical value.

It might be objected that the exercises suggested above do not, in strictness, appertain to the teaching of literature. But to this objection it may be replied that the study of the intellectual and logical aspects of the various forms of expression must necessarily fall within the province of the teacher of literature, and that, in any case, such teaching as we have here described would be more conveniently and appropriately included in the English course than in any other. It is true, however, that in this book our main interest in the various forms of expression must be in their literary and imaginative rather than in their strictly logical aspects, and we shall therefore now proceed to consider at greater length the rhetorical—the imaginative and emotional—aspects of the oration.

Even when a speaker's chief object may be to convince his audience of the truth of his propositions, and though his speech may be addressed mainly to the understanding, he generally seeks also to please the imagination, to influence the emotions and passions, and to move the will. If he is to persuade and stir his hearers effectively, he must appeal to their whole human nature, he must address them as beings capable not only of reasoning, but also of imagination and feeling and action. The orator's is a complex art, as the human nature to which he makes his appeal is complex. It is part of his equipment that he should be able to argue clearly and logically, so that he may lead his audience to adopt the beliefs and opinions which he advocates; and in the execution of this task he calls to his aid the imagination also, picturing vividly, by apt illustration and concrete instances, the actual and the ideal, what is and what ought to be; and he appeals, too, to the emotions and passions, which in turn influence the will and dispose his hearers' minds to action. Thus the intellect, the imagination, the emotions, and the will— the whole mental being of his audience—are the united objects of the speaker's attack : he seeks to convince the intellect, to charm the imagination, to excite the emotions and passions, and move the will.

An equal importance, however, is not always attached to the realisation of each of these aims. In some speeches the argumentative element may predominate; in others, the imaginative; and in others, again, the emotional. The orators of ancient Greece and Rome emphasised the emotional element considerably more than is usual in modern oratory. The political speeches of our own country and later times often emphasise rather the argumentative element. Professor Jebb[1] points out that many modern speeches consist for the most part in a succession of arguments, more or less closely inter-woven, intended in their combination primarily to convince the intellect. But in all real oratory, when a speaker is possessed by a sense of the truth and import of his utterance, or feels deeply that the gain of some moral or social purpose may depend on his words, the imaginative and emotional elements will be found to be organically fused with the logical element. The texture of his reasoning will then not only be sufficiently strong to capture and hold the hearer's understanding; it will also be illumined and coloured by the light of imagination and the glow of feeling.

In addressing himself to the imagination, a speaker often proceeds by the method of illustration: he may add vividness and variety by the use of comparison, contrast, anecdote, or the citation of particular cases and pathetic or humorous instances; and his language, too, will be concrete and suffused with imagery. The conditions under which a speech is delivered, and the speaker's relation to his audience, make it desirable, as a rule, that the subject-matter should be presented in a more immediately interesting and attractive style than in a book or essay; and by the illustrations and imagery of a speech most hearers are readily attracted.

The following passage from Burke's Speech on Conciliation with America may be quoted to illustrate the typical oratorical use of concrete terms and imagery.

---

[1] *The Attic Orators, from Antiphon to Isaeus.* By R. C. Jebb (Macmillan and Co).—Introduction.

Burke had argued that concession ought to be offered
to a country so populous and commercially important
as America; and to bring home to his audience the
importance of American commerce he proceeded to
describe some of its main activities. In the following
passage he speaks of the American fisheries:

..." Pass by the other parts, and look at the manner
in which the people of New England have of late
carried on the whale fishery. Whilst we follow them
among the tumbling mountains of ice, and behold them
penetrating into the deepest frozen recesses of Hudson's
Bay and Davis's Straits, whilst we are looking for them
beneath the arctic circle, we hear that they have
pierced into the opposite region of polar cold, that they
are at the antipodes, and engaged under the frozen
serpent of the south. Falkland Island, which seemed
too remote and romantic an object for the grasp of
national ambition, is but a stage and resting-place in
the progress of their victorious industry. Nor is the
equinoctial heat more discouraging to them than the
accumulated winter of both the poles. We know
that whilst some of them draw the line and strike the
harpoon on the coast of Africa, others run the longitude
and pursue their gigantic game along the coast of
Brazil. No sea but what is vexed by their fisheries.
No climate that is not witness to their toils. Neither
the perseverance of Holland, nor the activity of France,
nor the dexterous and firm sagacity of English enterprise ever carried this most perilous mode of hardy
industry to the extent to which it has been pushed by
this recent people—a people who are still, as it were,
but in the gristle, and not yet hardened into the bone

of manhood. When I contemplate these things, when I know that the colonies in general owe little or nothing to any care of ours, and that they are not squeezed into this happy form by the constraints of watchful and suspicious government, but that, through a wise and salutary neglect, a generous nature has been suffered to take her own way to perfection; when I reflect upon these effects, when I see how profitable they have been to us, I feel all the pride of power sink, and all presumption in the wisdom of human contrivances melt and die away within me. My rigour relents. I pardon something to the spirit of liberty."

The conclusion of this passage illustrates well the relation of the illustrative element in oratory to the logical element. An important feature in the composition of the speech-form is that illustrations and concrete instances are used by a speaker not merely to make his subject-matter clearer and more attractive, but also to justify and recommend the opinions or actions for which he is advocate—that is to say, practically as arguments. It is impossible to draw an absolute distinction between argument and illustration in oratory: they are closely related both in their essential nature and in their aims. Since, in general, the subject-matter with which the orator deals—be it political, social, legal, economic, moral, or religious—is really incalculable and infinitely complex, most of his arguments can demonstrate no scientific certainty, afford no absolute proof: they establish only a greater or a less degree of probability; and illustrations from example or from analogy, added, as they are, in some measure, to reinforce the arguments, may be said, from a rhetorical point of view, to have a certain amount of probative value.

The emotional element in speeches, like the imaginative, finds definite expression mainly in rhetorical figures—the former in figures of emotion, as the latter in figures of imagery. The character of the figures employed varies with the speaker's aim. If his primary aim be merely to expound clearly some plan or policy, the figures of speech will be of a more intellectual and imaginative cast; he will add clearness and point to his statement by a moderate use of antithesis, epigram, simile, and metaphor. But if he desires to excite strong feeling and arouse his hearers to action, he will call to his aid also the more striking and emotional figures—climax, apostrophe, interrogation, sarcasm, irony, denunciation, prediction, vision, appeal to God. In the speeches of our own time and country the emotional element is not, as a rule, so explicit or emphatic as in the oratory of the past or of other countries; yet it is always present in some degree, and must be present, whenever a speaker aims at moving men to action.

The following passage, taken from Lord Brougham's Speech on Negro Emancipation, illustrates the use of an imaginative and emotional figure that frequently occurs, though expressed, as a rule, in a less fervid form in modern speeches, viz., the figure of prediction or vision. In this quotation, as in the passage quoted above from Burke, the reader will note that the imaginative and emotional appeal produces also something of the effect of argument:

" From the instant that glad sound [the proclamation of complete emancipation] is wafted across the ocean, what a blessed change begins; what an enchanting prospect unfolds itself! The African, placed upon the same footing with other men, becomes in reality our fellow-citizen—to our feelings, as well as in his own nature, our equal, our brother....Where the driver and the gaoler once bore sway, the lash resounds no more, nor does the clank of the chain any more fall upon the troubled ear; the fetter has ceased to gall the vexed limb, and the very mark disappears which for a while it had left. All races and colours run together the same glorious race of improvement. Peace unbroken, harmony uninterrupted, calm unruffled, reigns in mansion and in field, in the busy street and the fertile valley, where nature, with the lavish hand she extends under the tropical sun, pours forth all her bounty profusely, because received in the lap of cheerful industry, not extorted by hands cramped with bonds. Delightful pictures of general prosperity and social progress in all the arts of civility and refinement!"

The concluding passage of this speech of Lord Brougham may be quoted as a striking example of the emotional style, though it must be admitted that its impassioned strains would not be likely to produce in a modern audience the precise effect intended by the speaker:

"The slave has shown, by four years' blameless behaviour and devotion to the pursuits of peaceful industry, that he is as fit for his freedom as any English peasant, aye, or any Lord whom I now address. I demand his rights; I demand his liberty without stint. In the name of justice and law, in the name of reason, in the name of God, who has given you no right to work injustice, I demand that your brother be no longer trampled upon as your slave! I make my appeal to the Commons, who represent the free people of England, and I require at their hands the performance of that condition for which they paid so enormous a price—that condition which all their constituents are in breathless anxiety to see fulfilled. I appeal to this House—hereditary judges of the first tribunal in the world, to you I appeal for justice! Patrons of all the arts that humanize mankind, under your protection I place humanity herself! To the merciful Sovereign of a free people, I call aloud for mercy to the hundreds of thousands for whom half a million of her Christian sisters have cried out; I ask that their cry may not have risen in vain. But first I turn my eye to the Throne of all justice, and devoutly humbling myself before Him who is of purer eyes than to behold such vast iniquities, I implore that the curse hovering over the head of the unjust and the oppressor be averted from us, that your hearts may be turned to mercy, and that over all the earth His will may at length be done."

By thus appealing to the emotions and passions a speaker aims at reinforcing his arguments, and, though it may seem paradoxical to say so, the process involved may be considered as a kind of reasoning. His aim often is to convince his hearers that the realisation of the policy he advocates will satisfy in them some right feeling or sentiment to which outrage is done by present actual conditions. The emotional appeal in oratory, like the imaginative, is closely allied to the logical and argumentative; and it may be said that the essential characteristic of the speech form consists precisely in this close fusion of the logical, the imaginative, and the emotional elements, and in the peculiar relation in which the two latter stand to the former.

The organic fusion and a characteristic interplay of those three elements it is that constitutes the true and complete oratorical appeal.

This thesis may be made clearer by a brief contrast of oratory and poetry, and of true and false rhetoric. The poet, like the orator, aims at persuasion ; and for this reason imagery, emotion, and illustrations of all kinds, literal and figurative, are characteristic alike of poetry and of oratory. But the orator, unlike the poet, has an immediately practical end in view : he seeks to convince his hearers of the truth of certain propositions, and to rouse them to action ; and his appeal to the imagination and emotions is legitimate only in so far as it is grounded in his logical and practical purpose. Thus if he excites in his audience a particular desire or passion, he should also satisfy their judgment that there is a connexion between the action to which he would persuade them and the gratification of that desire or passion. The poet has no such argumentative or immediately practical end in view ; his essential object, and the underlying principle on which he unconsciously or consciously works, is to impart a sense of beauty or grandeur and to give pleasure. This principle is the golden link that unites his subject-matter, and gives to it characteristic form; in poetry, one image or emotion leads naturally to another, and each is related to each by the principle of beauty or grandeur. But in oratory the link of connexion is of another and harder metal—as of steel rather than gold. Here sentence should follow sentence, and period period, linked by the demands of truth and the necessity of the argument. Whithersoever truth leads, there must the orator go. His way too, indeed, may be adorned with the flowers of rhetoric and passion, but they must be firmly rooted in the soil of his argument. The images and embellishments and the emotional colouring of his speech should aim essentially, not at imparting a sense of beauty or grandeur, but rather at adding force and clearness to the apprehension of truth that he desires to convey. Hazlitt, in one of his essays[1], says truly that Burke "always aims at overpowering rather than at pleasing; and consequently sacrifices beauty and delicacy to force and vividness. He has invariably a task to perform, a positive purpose to execute, an effect to produce. His only object is therefore to strike hard, and in the right place; if he misses his mark, he repeats his blow; and does not care how ungraceful the action, or how clumsy the instrument, provided it brings down his antagonist." And in another essay[2] Hazlitt remarks that Burke's style "may be said to pass yawning gulfs 'on the unsteadfast footing of a spear': still, it has an actual resting-place and tangible support under it—it is not suspended on nothing. It differs from poetry, as I conceive, like the chamois from the eagle: it climbs to an almost equal height, touches upon a cloud, overlooks a precipice, is picturesque, sublime—but all the while, instead of soaring through the air, it stands upon a rocky cliff, clambers up by abrupt and intricate ways, and browses on the roughest bark, or crops the tender flower."

[1] " Character of Mr Burke."
[2] " On the Prose Style of Poets."

The method of the false rhetorician is different. Merely to attract and please, he will drag in illustrations and anecdotes that have no real connexion with the argument, and employ meretricious images and figures of speech that dazzle his hearers' minds and obscure right judgment. He will appeal to the personal interests of his audience, and to their more ignoble passions, as party spirit and class animosity, without regard to the nature of the question at issue. He will substitute for reasoned conclusions bold affirmations, and be at no pains to establish any connexion between the conduct he urges and the end proposed. The organic fusion that should subsist between the argumentative and the imaginative and emotional elements in oratory is absent from his speeches.

Applying the preceding remarks from a more immediately pedagogic point of view, let us now consider how, in studying a speech, we would approach a characteristic rhetorical passage, to what features we should direct our pupils' attention, and what questions we should ask. The following from one of John Bright's Speeches[1] may be cited :

" We all know and deplore that at the present moment a large number of the grown men of Europe are employed, and a large portion of the industry of Europe is absorbed, to provide for, and maintain, the enormous armaments which are now on foot in every considerable Continental State....I believe that I understate the sum when I say that, in pursuit of this will-o'-the-wisp [the liberties of Europe and the balance of power], there has been extracted from the industry of

[1] " On Foreign Policy," Birmingham.

the people of this small island no less an amount than
£2,000,000,000 sterling....When I try to think of that
sum of £2,000,000,000, there is a sort of vision passes
before my mind's eye. I see your peasant labourer
delve and plough, sow and reap, sweat beneath the
summer's sun, or grow prematurely old before the
winter's blast. I see your noble mechanic, with his
manly countenance and his matchless skill, toiling at
his bench or his forge. I see one of the workers in our
factories in the north, a woman—a girl, it may be—
gentle and good, as many of them are, as your sisters
and daughters are—I see her intent upon the spindle,
whose revolutions are so rapid that the eye fails altogether to detect them, or watching the alternating
flight of the unresting shuttle. I turn again to another
portion of your population, which, 'plunged in mines,
forgets a sun was made,' and I see the man who
brings up from the secret chambers of the earth the
elements of the riches and greatness of his country.
When I see all this I have before me a mass of produce
and of wealth which I am no more able to comprehend
than I am that £2,000,000,000 of which I have spoken,
but I behold in its full proportions the hideous error of
your Governments, whose fatal policy consumes in some
cases a half, never less than a third, of all the results
of that industry which God intended should fertilise
and bless every home in England, but the fruits of
which are squandered in every part of the surface of
the globe, without producing the smallest good to the
people of England."

In the study of this passage a pupil might first be
asked to state the main proposition it advances—viz.,

that "a large portion of the industry of Europe is
absorbed to provide for enormous armaments." This
proposition the speaker proceeds to elaborate and
enliven by expressing it in terms of imagination and
feeling. What illustrations, then, precisely are employed,
and to what emotions does he appeal ? Illustration by
examples is prominent in the passage, the rhetorical
figure of " vision " occurs, and the sentiments of justice,
pity, anger, and self-interest are evoked. Having
referred in general terms to " the industry of Europe,"
the speaker applies his proposition more particularly to
the case of England. In this application there is an
underlying appeal to the feelings of his audience, for
people regard with more emotion the conditions that
affect their own lives than those that affect the in-
habitants of other countries. To bring his proposition
home to the business and bosoms of his audience, John
Bright goes on to translate the abstract notion of the
industry of England into the concrete. With a few
strokes he produces a series of vivid and individualised
pictures representing the peasant labourer, the mechanic,
the factory worker, and the miner as if he saw them at
the moment in the performance of their labours. What
is the mental effect produced by this figure of vision ?
And involved in this process of illustration there is a
subtle appeal to his hearers' interests and to their sense
of pity and justice. What details show this? The working
classes of England are industrious and their lot is a
hard one—the peasant "sweats beneath the summer's
sun or grows prematurely old before the winter's blast,"
the "noble mechanic " toils at his bench and forge, the
miner may easily " forget a sun was made," yet they do

not reap the just reward of their labours—the fruits of their industry " are squandered in every part of the surface of the globe without producing the smallest good to the people of England." Are these images and emotions evoked, then, by the speaker for their own sake or merely to attract and excite his hearers ? By no means. They are closely related to the main argument of the whole speech; they are deliberately calculated to lead to such action on the part of the audience as may put an end to that foreign policy of war and expansion which Bright condemned.

Take, again, the following passage from Lord Brougham's speech on Negro Emancipation:

"Ask you if crimes like these, murderous in their legal nature, as well as frightful in their aspect, passed unnoticed ; if enquiry was neglected to be made respecting those deaths in a prison ? No such thing ! The forms of justice were on this head peremptory even in the West Indies, and those forms, the handmaids of justice, were present, though their sacred mistress was far away. The coroner duly attended, his jury were regularly empanelled ; eleven inquisitions were made in order, and eleven verdicts returned. Murder ? Manslaughter ? Misdemeanour ? Misconduct? No ; but 'Died by the visitation of God.' Died by the visitation of God ! A lie ! a perjury ! a blasphemy ! The visitation of God ! Yes ; for it is among the most awful of these visitations by which the inscrutable purposes of His will are mysteriously accomplished that He sometimes arms the wicked with power to oppress the guiltless; and if there be any visitation more dreadful than another—any which more tries the faith and vexes the reason of erring mortals—it is when Heaven showers down upon the earth the plague, not of scorpions, or pestilence, or famine, or war, but of unjust judges or perjured jurors—wretches who pervert the law to wreak their personal vengeance or compass their sordid ends, and forswear themselves on the gospels of God, to the end that injustice may prevail, and the innocent be destroyed."

Here the emotional element is dominant. How does it display itself? The speaker appeals to his hearers' sense of justice and responsibility, and seeks to arouse their indignation. But this emotional element is grounded in, and rises out of, the main argument, which is to the effect that slavery should be abolished, since it involves inhumanity and gross cruelty. To show that slavery has led to acts of cruelty, Lord Brougham cites the particular case of eleven slaves who had died in prison. But the bare, logical statement of his argument would not produce the effect at which the speaker aims. That he should succeed in conveying the mere intellectual apprehension that slavery involves cruelty does not satisfy him. He will so speak that the whole being of his hearers shall realise the situation vividly and feel it deeply and rise up in revolt against it. The form of his expression is consonant with his purpose. What are the rhetorical figures employed? What mental effect is produced by interrogation, by exclamation, by climax (e.g., "a lie, a perjury, a blasphemy")?

Sufficient may now have been said to show that the oration is in itself a highly interesting form of expression, and that it may serve as a valuable medium for the introduction of our pupils to the study of argument, illustration, figurative expression, and emotion in speech. Through the concrete instances of argument that it affords, the principles of logic as applied to discourse may be studied; in it, too, something may be learnt of the emotions and sentiments by which the actions and lives of men are swayed. It contains, implicitly, the material of a kind of informal psychology, and, as a form of expression, it possesses unique characteristics. For those reasons we may fairly claim that it should receive a more detailed and careful consideration in our Secondary and Continuation Schools than has been given to it hitherto.

CHAPTER IX.

THE DESCRIPTIVE TOUCH AND IMAGERY IN THE TEACHING OF LITERATURE.

ONE of the chief characteristics of imaginative literature as regards its diction is that it prefers a concrete to an abstract mode of expression : it avoids the expression of general and vague ideas, and uses words and phrases that appeal to the reader's imagination and aesthetic sense by calling up a defined image or picture. This circumstance accounts for the frequent use of descriptive epithets, similes, and metaphors in imaginative literature. So prominent and important are these features that every teacher of literature should study carefully how he may best suggest to his pupils a sense of right appreciation with regard to them. If his teaching in this respect be successful, he will have gone far towards enabling his pupils truly to enjoy the reading of the best authors.

From time to time, then, in the study of certain suitable passages, the teacher may have in view as his main object the illustration of what may be described generally as the descriptive touch in literature. The books that are best adapted for teaching of this kind are, for the most part, books of poetry and imaginative prose. The method that should be adopted is, essentially, that of suggestion by the teacher and discovery by the pupil. And the chief particular points upon which the method may be concentrated are instances of descriptive epithets, similes, and metaphors.

The following passages from Stevenson's *The Black Arrow* may be cited as furnishing material for the treatment here indicated :

"They awoke in the grey of the morning ; the birds were not yet in full song, but twittered here and there among the woods; the sun was not yet up, but the eastern sky was barred with solemn colours."

"The short winter's day was near an end ; the sun, a dull red orange, shorn of rays, swam low among the leafless thickets."

"Upon the very margin of the ditch, not thirty feet from where they crouched, an iron cauldron bubbled and steamed above a glowing fire; and close by, in an attitude of listening, as though he had caught some sound of their clambering among the ruins, a tall, red-faced, battered-looking man stood poised, an iron spoon in his right hand, a horn and a formidable dagger at his belt. Plainly this was the singer ; plainly he had been stirring the cauldron, when some incautious step among the lumber had fallen upon his ear. A little further off another man lay slumbering, rolled in a brown cloak, with a butterfly hovering above his face. All this was in a clearing white with daisies; and at the extreme verge a bow, a sheaf of arrows, and part of a deer's carcase, hung upon a flowering hawthorn."

" An arrow sang in the air, like a huge hornet."

" One of his retainers led up a poor, cringing old man, as pale as a candle, and all shaking with the fen fever."

" They made but poor speed of it by now, labouring dismally as they ran, and catching for their breath like fish."

" The kitchen roared with cookery like a bees' hive."

In the illustration of descriptive detail direct and didactic teaching should be avoided ; the teacher would fail in his object if he were to point out to the class specially expressive or pictorial words and phrases, and remark on their descriptive quality. As the art of literature is marked by reticence and delicacy, so too is the right method of teaching literature.

At the end of a paragraph the question may be put to the class generally : " What words or phrases or sentences appeal to you as being particularly expressive, and as calling up a vivid picture before you ? "

Some of the answers given may be discussed, more or less fully, with the pupils. Suppose, for instance, that a pupil had expressed a preference for the first paragraph cited above—the description of sunrise in the woods. The teacher, after approving of the selection, might ask the pupil to name the details that seemed to him to make the picture expressive. The grey colour of the sky, the fitful twittering of the birds, and the solemn colours of the East might be mentioned in the reply. The epithet " solemn " would call for special enquiry. What colours may be appropriately described as " solemn " ? Red and purple were named in class as instances of such colours. One pupil associated them with the stained-glass windows in a cathedral or church, and another associated purple with the robes assumed by kings on solemn occasions.   The third paragraph is full of descriptive touches. The pupils, when asked to give details suggestive of the general appearance and the stillness of the scene, mentioned the clearing white with daisies, the flowering hawthorn, and the figure of the sleeping man with the butterfly hovering over his face. The red-faced listening man, the cauldron, and the deer's carcase were also given as examples of descriptive detail filling up the picture.

An important feature in the art of description, as it is illustrated in the best writers, is the economy of the means used to produce a pictorial effect. A single adjective or phrase, an expressive verb, a short, appropriate simile, or a combination of the three serves to suggest to the reader a complete mental picture; as in the nervous phrases of Stevenson: "An arrow sang in the air like a huge hornet"; "The kitchen roared with cookery like a bees' hive"; "One of his retainers led up a poor, cringing old man, as pale as a candle, and all shaking with the fen fever." Occasionally the teacher may suggest this characteristic to his pupils, even by such a mechanical means as asking them to state the number of words that comprise the description.

After a few informal lessons of this kind have been given, exercises may be set, so that the pupils may have an opportunity of applying the teaching and using their powers of fancy and imagination. Such exercises as the following are generally found interesting:

(1) Find suitable comparisons for: (*a*) the sun setting over the sea; (*b*) the sun rising over hills; (*c*) a stormy sea; (*d*) a fallen tree; (*e*) an ugly giant and a beautiful child; (*f*) the daisy; (*g*) a lake by night; (*h*) trees moved by the wind; (*i*) men panting in a race; (*j*) an arrow whizzing through the air.

(2) Write a short description, so as to convey a vivid mental picture, of the following (the first four subjects are based on the opening passages of *The Lay of the Last Minstrel*): (*a*) a Border Tower; (*b*) the Last Minstrel; (*c*) the Minstrel's melody; (*d*) the streets of Edinburgh when the Chief of Branksome fell; (*e*) a grove of trees; (*f*) almond blossom; (*g*) an omnibus; (*h*) a shop window.

The following is a selection from the best answers submitted to the above questions in a class (of the average age of fourteen) in a boys' secondary school:

"The waves of the sea flashed like bayonets in the Afric sun." "The golden sun, like Phoebus' chariot descending the hill, set flashing o'er the sea." "The sun was setting and leaving the earth, like a soul that, having done its work on earth, goes to other regions, leaving behind it a long pathway of its good deeds."

"The stormy sea was washing the decks of the derelict like a hungry monster playing with its prey before devouring it." "The sea was tossing like a drove of wild horses, and the foam flying on its billows was like their manes."

"The ugly giant and the beautiful child look like evil and good personified." "There they stood, a cherub from Heaven and a denizen of Hell." "The ugly giant looked like the personification of evil, while the beautiful child looked like a lovely lily."

"The jeweller's windows were brilliantly illuminated with electric light, making the gems glisten and sparkle like fire-flies. Here were diamonds, there opals and every other gem mentionable, each seeming to outshine the others in its brilliancy."

" The soft, pink almond-blossom has given way before the boisterous March winds, and now the ground is covered with its dainty petals. The almond-tree sighs to the wind, for it is loth to part so soon with its glory."

The errors made by the pupils in writing such exercises enable the teacher to give some valuable lessons in the art of correct and delicate literary expression. Instances suitable for this purpose may be copied on the blackboard, and the pupils' attention called to the mistakes that the sentences illustrate.

The most common error in this particular set of exercises consisted in the use of words or phrases not harmonising with the context. This was especially noticeable in the instances of similes. Thus one pupil wrote : " The sun was rising in the hills like a gigantic orange, growing stronger as it rose, and clearing away the mist by which it was surrounded." Another wrote : " An ugly giant and a beautiful child seem to be like a demon and an angel, the one hovering near to do wrong, the other to do good." The question was put : "What word in the sentence is inappropriate ? " The word " hovering " was cited, and the pupil who gave the answer added as his reason that we may not justly speak of a giant as " hovering." It was then pointed out that when we use comparisons or similes we should not attempt to give too much detail : if the writers of those two sentences had stopped respectively after the words " orange " and " angel," the expression would have been at least correct ; in the use of such figures of speech every detail that is added makes it more difficult for the writer to sustain the correspondence of the whole comparison.

Another defect that occurred in the exercises was the use of commonplace or inappropriate comparisons. Here the imagination of the pupil was at fault. The following are instances : " The panting of a man is like the panting of a dog " ; " the panting man's chest rose and fell like the ripples on the sea-shore " ; " the rising of the sun was like the rays of a lamp." In connection with such faulty comparisons the teacher may discuss with the pupils the *object* that a writer usually has in view in using similes and comparisons : his object, generally, is to add vividness and interest to the ideas or images that he seeks to express. Similes that do not achieve that purpose are not only useless, and add nothing to the expression, they are actual faults in style, diverting the reader's attention unnecessarily from the main idea or image that should be in view, and so making the subject less clear and interesting than it would be if it were expressed in a simpler and more direct form. For example, if we say " the panting of a man is like the panting of a dog," no real purpose is served by such a comparison : the resemblance suggested is between two things of the same kind, and is obvious and commonplace. On the other hand, if the likeness suggested is too remote or too laboured, again the simile is faulty, as in the following : " A railway-station is like the centre of a circle, the railway itself connecting it with the outer world, and the passengers coming in and going out being the radii." Such a comparison makes the subject less instead of more intelligible.

After some practice and discussion on those lines, the pupils may be asked to supply suitable images to complete the sense of passages taken from a book not previously known to them. For instance, in the class to which we have referred, some passages from George Eliot's *Silas Marner* were read and written to dictation —the similes occurring in the passages being omitted, and the pupils asked to fill in suitable images. It was explained that the comparisons supplied should be with common objects, and such as might naturally suggest themselves to the characters speaking. The following is copied verbatim from one of the exercises submitted (the comparisons supplied by the pupil are italicised):

SIMILES FROM *SILAS MARNER*
(GEORGE ELIOT).

Complete the similes in the following passages :

Villagers' Conversation at a Dance.

(1) " ' The Squire's pretty springe, considering his weight,' said Mr Macey, ' and he stamps uncommon well. But Mr Lammeter beats 'em all for shapes : you see, he holds his head *like that stout old Colonel what we see t'other marnin'*, and he isn't so cushiony as most o' the oldish gentlefolks—they run fat in general.' "

(2) " ' Talk o' nimbleness, look at Mrs Osgood,' said Ben Winthrop, who was holding his son Aaron between his knees. ' She trips along with her little steps, so as nobody can see how she goes—it's *like as if she was our wench runnin' from the coo' after milkin' 'er*.' "

(3) " ' Fayder,' said Aaron, whose feet were busy beating out the tune, ' how does that big cock's-feather stick in Mrs Crackenthorp's yead ? Is there a little hole for it, like in my shuttlecock ? '

' Hush, lad, hush ; that's the way the ladies dress

theirselves, that is,' said the father, adding, however, in an undertone to Mr Macey, ' it does make her look funny, though—partly like *that there Bornyo savage what come round with the circus last year*. Hey, by jingo, there's the young Squire leading off now, wi' Miss Nancy for partners. There's a lass for you!— like *a lily of the valley*! There's nobody 'ud think as anybody could be so pritty.'"

(4) [*Describing a changeable character, Master Godfrey*.] "'One while he was allays after Miss Nancy, and then it all went off again, like *a wacillating wane— first this way, then t'other*, as I may say. That wasn't my way when *I* went a-coorting.'

'Ah, but mayhap Miss Nancy hung off, like, and your lass didn't,' said Ben.

'I should say she didn't,' said Mr Macey significantly. ' Before I said "sniff," I took care to know as she'd say "snaff," and pretty quick too. I wasn't a-going to open *my* mouth, like *a fish at a fly*, and snap it to again, wi' nothing to swaller.'"

When these exercises were returned the similes used by George Eliot were told to the class, as follows : (1) " like a sodger " ; (2) " it's like as if she had little wheels to her feet " ; (3) " partly like a short-necked bottle wi' a long quill in it " ; " like a pink-and-white posy " ; (4) " like a smell o' hot porridge " ; " like a dog at a fly." The pupils were interested in comparing their own attempts with the original similes, the brevity and naturalness of which the teacher was thus enabled to emphasise.

In poetry the use of descriptive epithets and of similes and metaphors is still more prominent than in

imaginative prose ; but, whether in poetry or in prose,
the object of their use is to increase the vividness or
the interest of the ideas or images expressed.   It is
better, as a rule, to avoid the formal analysis, in written
exercises, of imaginative comparisons used in poetry, but
it is a good plan sometimes to discuss informally the
suggestiveness and appropriateness of certain similes and
metaphors. By such discussion, for instance, in the reading
of the *Morte d'Arthur*, pupils might be led to discover for
themselves the pictorial significance and expressiveness
of these passages :

> " The great brand
> Made lightnings in the splendour of the moon,
> And flashing round and round, and whirl'd in an arch,
> Shot *like a streamer of the northern morn.*"

> " All the decks were dense with stately forms
> Black-stoled, black-hooded, *like a dream.*"

> " So, *like a shatter'd column*, lay the King."

> " Wherefore, let thy voice
> Rise *like a fountain* for me night and day."

In view, then, of the importance in creative literature
generally of epithets, similes, and metaphors, it should
be considered an essential point to enable the pupil to
regard them from the right point of view and to appreciate
them rightly.   And such teaching is justified, not only
because of its importance in relation to the subject-
matter and treatment of literature, but because of the
special interest that it arouses in the pupil. The young
have a far keener appreciation of the concrete and pictorial than of the abstract and reflective. At the
suggestion of a clear-cut and coloured picture their

intelligence brightens, and the relation between literature and life is implicitly perceived. Through such suggestive teaching as has been indicated the pupil's whole view of life may unconsciously be coloured. He may be prepared gradually to see the world as a place not of one uniform tint or atmosphere, but of many lights and shadows, the perception of which will add to the interest and charm of our lives. The suggestive treatment of epithets, similes, and metaphors in the teaching of literature finds its final justification in the circumstance that these express, in a manner fitted to appeal strongly to our pupils, the various and changing aspects of living reality.

CHAPTER X.

READING ALOUD AND LITERARY APPRECIATION.

IF one were asked to sum up in a word the most characteristic and essential quality in the work of the creative literary artist, one would be inclined to reply : " atmosphere." In reading certain books we feel that the writer has created a new and distinctive atmosphere in which, for the time being, we live; and our capacity for appreciating literature is proportionate to our capacity for breathing the characteristic atmosphere thus created. One of the teacher's primary aims must be so to deal with his subject that his pupils may breathe, and be inspired by, the imaginative atmosphere of the literature they read.

For the attainment of this end one of the most valuable means that can be employed is reading aloud. In these pages we have been concerned more particularly with the intensive study of literature; but very often it is unnecessary, or would be pernicious, to use the intensive method : in dealing with many simple lyric poems, for instance, we ought to avoid detailed treatment and rely mainly on the expressive reading aloud of the poems. As a rule, the younger our pupils, the less detailed should be our treatment. But, whatever the age of the pupils may be, it is always necessary that the teacher should himself feel the characteristic imaginative charm of the passages or books studied and should seek to communicate it; and for this reason reading aloud, which is one of the best means of suggesting a sense of atmosphere, is appropriate at all stages of the curriculum.

It is now recognised that every teacher of literature ought to be able to read aloud expressively. By the teacher's reading, often, more easily and naturally than by any other means, the pupils will be led to appreciate rightly the distinctive tone of a passage in prose or verse. And there are times, too, when it is no less important that the pupils themselves should read aloud. The relative importance that should be attached to the teacher's and the pupil's reading will vary with circumstances. In junior classes the teacher will depend more upon his own expressive reading to suggest the tone or atmosphere of the passages read. Again, in the study of poetry generally, or of literature that is permeated by a subtle imaginative charm, the teacher's reading will assume more relative importance. Many young children themselves know that they cannot render adequately in their reading the charm of fine poetry. This does not mean that they are incapable of appreciating it; on the contrary, the fact that they thus feel their own limitations would seem to indicate rather a capacity for literary appreciation: what is lacking in such pupils is not appreciation, but the technical equipment necessary for its expression in reading. The reading aloud of fiction, on the other hand, and of most prose literature, should generally be done by the pupils themselves; and in the study of plays, again, at all stages, it is essential that the pupils should themselves do the reading and acting—with this topic we shall deal more fully below[1].

It can form no part of the scheme of this chapter to discuss in detail the conditions of expressive reading, but it will be necessary to refer to certain aspects of the subject, with a view to illustrating, presently, by reference to particular passages, how reading aloud may be used as a means of expressing meaning, suggesting atmosphere, and promoting literary appreciation.

Considered from a physical point of view, reading aloud consists in the production by the human voice of a series of significant sounds. These sounds, taken singly and together, are marked by various shades and degrees of expressiveness and melody, and this variety is employed in literature to produce in the hearer or reader particular mental effects. The most obvious use of this capacity of speech sounds occurs in the imitation of natural sounds (onomatopoeia). Some writers go so far as to assert that every speech sound has a distinct and special meaning. Whether this assertion be true or not, it is at least an admitted fact that certain sounds uttered by the human voice are in themselves expressive of certain feelings. For instance, as Professor Sweet has pointed out, " primitive man probably expressed sensual enjoyment generally, as some of us still do, by an inbreathed voiceless l." And an American professor (Prof. MacClintock, of Chicago University, writing on "Literature in the Elementary School") says that "anyone who knows children will have noticed the pleasure that the merest babies will take in beautiful or especially pat collocations of syllables. A child whom

[1] v. inf., pp. 160—163.

I knew, just beginning to talk, would say to himself many times a day, and always with a smile of amused pleasure, the phrases, 'apple-batter pudding,' 'piccalilli pickles,' 'up into the cherry-tree,' 'piping down the valleys wild.' It is probably true that some of his apparent pleasure was that species of hysteria produced in most babies by any mild explosion, and the little fusillade of p's in the examples he liked best would account for a part of his enjoyment. But we must think that there was pleasure there, and whether it was physical or mental, it arose from the pleasing combination of verbal sounds."

This " pleasing combination of verbal sounds" is characteristic of all good literature. " Each phrase in literature," says R. L. Stevenson in a notable passage, " is built of sounds, as each phrase in music consists of notes. One sound suggests, echoes, demands, and harmonises with another; and the art of rightly using these concordances is the final art in literature....The beauty of the contents of a phrase, or of a sentence, depends implicitly upon alliteration and upon assonance. The vowel demands to be repeated; the consonant demands to be repeated; and both cry aloud to be perpetually varied. You may follow the adventures of a letter through any passage that has particularly pleased you ; find it, perhaps, denied a while, to tantalise the ear ; find it fired again at you in a whole broadside ; or find it pass into congenerous sounds, one liquid or labial melting away into another. And you will find another and much stranger circumstance. Literature is written by and for two senses: a sort of internal ear, quick to perceive ' unheard melodies ' ; and the eye,

which directs the pen and deciphers the printed phrase.
Well, even as there are rhymes for the eye, so you will
find that there are assonances and alliterations; that
where an author is running the open A, deceived by the
eye and our strange English spelling, he will often show
a tenderness for the flat A; and that where he is running a particular consonant, he will not improbably
rejoice to write it down even when it is mute or bears
a different value [1]."

It is important, then, for literary appreciation that
we should be able to perceive the aesthetic effects
produced by sounds, taken singly and in their various
successions and combinations. The study of phonetics
has an important bearing not only on the art of reading
clearly, reading so that we may be understood, but also
on the art of reading expressively, so that we may convey
a certain tone of feeling. Even from the most elementary
phonetic distinctions—as, for example, from the fundamental classification of speech sounds into vowels and
consonants—we may learn valuable lessons in the art
of expressive reading.

The classification of all verbal sounds as vowels or
consonants is based on the wider classification of sounds
into "noises" and "musical sounds." "All single sounds,"
says Mr Daniel Jones in his book on *The Pronunciation
of English* [2], "which consist entirely of noise, or a
combination of noise and voice, in which the noise
predominates, are called consonants. The sound of the

[1] *Essays in the Art of Writing.* By R. L. Stevenson. Chatto and
Windus: 1910.

[2] *The Pronunciation of English.* By Daniel Jones, M.A. Cambridge:
at the University Press, 1911.

voice issuing from the mouth without the addition of any perceptible noise, constitutes a vowel." In general, then, it is the vowel-sounds that form the musical element in speech; and the superiority in melody of one language over another will be proportionate to the greater number and variety, and the more musical quality, of its vowel-sounds. At the same time, it must also be remembered that many of the consonants also have a musical quality.

The elementary phonetic distinction drawn between vowels and consonants points to the conclusion that in the reading aloud of literature, and especially of poetry, in which the element of music plays an important part, special attention should be given to the enunciation of the vowel-sounds, which are the more musical. If, as we read, we realise and render adequately the characteristic musical effect of each of the vowel-sounds and diphthongs, our reading will be more effective. In reading poetry of a serious or lofty character, especially, a good elocutionist generally takes care to prolong the vowel-sounds, giving them their full musical value. And it may be added that this prolongation of the vowel-sounds in the reading of poetry is desirable not only in order that the musical effect may be heightened, but also that the meaning may be conveyed more clearly. Prose is in its essential nature a more diffuse form of expression than poetry, which is marked by a certain closeness of texture : the breath-groups in poetry are shorter, and the sense is more condensed. To give the hearer time, therefore, to apprehend the more pregnant significance, as well as to render adequately the music, of a serious poetical passage, it should usually be read more deliberately than prose.

Each of the vowel-sounds, too, possesses a distinctive tone-character. Those that are associated with the deepest tones produce a coarser, a more voluminous or massive, effect, while those associated with the highest tones produce a thinner, more pointed and piercing, effect. Thus the vowel-sound *u*: (oo), associated with deep tones, has a more voluminous and massive quality than the sounds of *o* (oh), *ɔ*: (aw), *a* (ah), *e* (ay), or *i*: (ee), and this quality decreases progressively in the vowel-sounds in the order named, while on the other hand the sounds in this order produce an increasing sense of thinness and pointedness [1].

In serious, solemn, and exalted poetry the more massive vowel-sounds, such as *oo* and *oh*, occur more frequently than in lighter verse, in which the thinner vowel-sounds, such as *ay* and *ee*, predominate. This fact may be verified by examining in detail a number of passages opposed to one another in feeling and tone, and comparing them in respect of their vowel-sounds. The following two passages may be cited here to illustrate the general nature of the results demonstrated by such an investigation. For the purpose of our enquiry, the vowel-sounds may be divided into three classes: (1) Massive or voluminous: *u*: (as in f*oo*d), *o* (as in l*ow*), *u* (g*oo*d), ∧ (m*u*ch); (2) Intermediate: *ɔ*: (s*aw*), *a*: (f*a*ther), *a* (c*ow*), a (fl*y*), *ə*: (b*i*rd), *ɔ* (l*o*ng), *æ* (c*a*b), *ə* (*a*bove); (3) Thin or pointed: e (th*e*re), i: (qu*ee*n), *ɛ* (r*e*d), i (l*i*ft). In the tables given below, the diphthongs are analysed into their constituent sounds.

[1] Cf. Dr Myers's *Text Book of Experimental Psychology* (Vol. i, pp. 32, 33). Cambridge University Press.

I. HUNTING SONG.

Waken, lords and ladies gay,
On the mountain dawns the day,
All the jolly chase is here,
With hawk, and horse, and hunting-spear ;
Hounds are in their couples yelling,
Hawks are whistling, horns are knelling,
Merrily, merrily, mingle they,
" Waken, lords and ladies gay."

Waken, lords and ladies gay,
The mist has left the mountain grey,
Springlets in the dawn are steaming,
Diamonds on the brake are gleaming ;
And foresters have busy been,
To track the buck in thicket green ;
Now we come to chant our lay,
" Waken, lords and ladies gay. "

SCOTT.

The tone of these verses is light and lively, and an analysis of the vowel-sounds gives the following result :

	Class 1 Massive or Voluminous		Class 2 Intermediate			Class 3 Thin or Pointed	
Vowel Sounds	u:	o	ɔ:	a:, a, a	ə:	ɛ	i:
Number of	none	none	10	12	none	1	5
Vowel Sounds	u	ʌ	ɔ	æ	ə	e	i
Number of	5	4	4	1	30	23	51

Total number of vowel-sounds : 146

$$\text{Class 1: } 9 = 6·16°/_{o}$$
$$\text{,, } 2: 57 = 39·04 °/_{o}$$
$$\text{,, } 3: 80 = 54·79 °/_{o}$$

The thin vowel-sounds of Class 3 are nine times as numerous as those of Class 1 ; they are more numerous than Classes 1 and 2 added together.

II. *From* ODE ON THE DEATH OF WELLINGTON.

> Lead out the pageant : sad and slow,
> As fits an universal woe,
> Let the long long procession go,
> And let the sorrowing crowd about it grow,
> And let the mournful martial music blow ;
> The last great Englishman is low.

TENNYSON.

	Class 1 Massive or Voluminous		Class 2 Intermediate			Class 3 Thin or Pointed	
Vowel Sounds	uː	o	ɔː	*aː, a,* ɑ	əː	ɛ	iː
Number of	none	9	3	5	none	1	1
Vowel Sounds	u	ʌ	ɔ	æ	ə	e	i
Number of	5	none	none	3	8	4	8

Total number of vowel-sounds : 47

Class 1 : 14 = 29·78 °/$_\circ$
,,   2 : 19 = 40·42 °/$_\circ$
,,   3 : 14 = 29·78 °/$_\circ$

A comparison of the two passages in respect of the vowel-sounds gives, therefore, the following result :

	Class 1 Massive or Voluminous	Class 2 Intermediate	Class 3 Thin or Pointed
Hunting Song (Light and lively in tone)	6·16 °/$_\circ$	39·04 °/$_\circ$	54·79 °/$_\circ$
Ode (Sad and solemn in tone)	29·78 °/$_\circ$	40·42 °/$_\circ$	29·78 °/$_\circ$

This result is sufficiently striking, and it is typical of the results that the writer obtained in the course of a much more extensive investigation. The experiment demonstrated conclusively that the vowel-sounds in poetry tend to vary in character according to the meaning and tone.

A study of the characteristic differences between the various vowels—differences of sonority and of quantity as well as of massiveness—will help us, in reading, to give to each its appropriate value and so to express more fully and subtly the character or tone of the passage read.

The consonant-sounds, also, vary in character, and are used in literature to produce varying mental effects. Thus voiced consonants are more sonorous than breathed consonants, and voiced liquid consonants than other voiced consonants. The liquid *l* has a peculiar musical quality, and the same may be said, in a lesser degree, of the nasal consonants *m*, *n*, and *ng*, especially when they are combined with the rounded vowels of o in snow or oo in moon, or with such open vowels as a in man, o in long, etc. By prolonging slightly the sounds of those consonants we may add much to their musical effect. In the following verse from Dryden's *Song for St Cecilia's Day*, *r* and the nasal consonants are used expressively, and onomatopoeia also occurs:

> The double double double beat
>   Of the thuNdeRing dRuM
> CRies 'HaRk! the foes coMe;
>   ChaRge, chaRge, 'tis too late to RetReat!'

The fricatives, s, z, f, v, h, may also be used with characteristic effect. Thus *s* sometimes expresses appropriately a sense of hush and calm, and it therefore occurs frequently in poems about sleep; at other times it may be used to convey the sound of running water or breaking waves; and h may be employed to suggest the idea of continuous labour or effort, as in the well-known line: "Up a high hill he heaved a huge round stone." Further, apart from their suggestiveness individually, the consonants may, as Stevenson has pointed out, be varied and repeated in a paragraph or verse so as to add to its musical quality: he quotes the following as an example:

> The BaRge she sat iN, like a BURNished throNe
> BURNt oN the water: the PooP was BeateN gold,
> PURPle the sails and so PURFumèd that
> The wiNds were love-sick with them.

It has been thought advisable to dwell thus at considerable length on the musical quality of literature, and on the correspondence between sound and sense, in the first place because only if we have studied those matters in detail shall we be able to read aloud with full effect, and secondly because this factor in literary appreciation is often neglected.

Of the other conditions on which expressive reading depends, the most important are: the pitch and modulation of the voice; the intensity of the voice—that is, the loudness or softness of the musical tones employed; the pace of utterance, quick or slow; the varying emphasis laid on certain words and sentences; and pause. In the regulation of those details we should always be guided by the meaning and tone of the passage to be read. Having asked ourselves the question: What is the emotion or feeling intended? we should, in our reading, regulate the pitch, pace, pauses, emphasis, and degree of loudness so as to suit the emotion or feeling.

Thus, if a reader did not wish to awaken any special sentiment in his audience, he would employ the middle pitch of the voice; or if he were reading a comparatively unimportant, or a parenthetic, or an explanatory, statement, he would usually lower the pitch ; while if he wished to express earnestness he would raise the pitch. It is useful to remember that raising the pitch generally has the effect of elevating the hearers' spirits, while lowering the pitch tends to depress the spirits. In reading, as in speaking, the pitch of the voice should be constantly changing in correspondence with the meaning and emotion we seek to convey. To those variations in pitch the name of "intonation" or "inflection" is given; and they are used in the reading of words, phrases, clauses, and sentences to mark subordinate groups and to suggest varying emotion and emphasis. Three chief kinds of inflection are generally recognised : the rising, the falling, and the level. The rising inflection may express incompleteness, negation, indecision, and is used in questions that can be answered by "yes" or "no"; while the falling inflection expresses completeness, affirmation, decision, and is used in questions that cannot be answered by "yes" or "no." But no absolutely precise or invariable rules can be formulated on the subject : all that can be said is, in general terms, that the best inflection of the voice is that which expresses best the meaning and emotion intended.

In the reading of a short complete composition, by regulating the pitch and intensity of the voice, and the pace of utterance, we may sometimes be enabled to convey to our hearers a sense not only of the varying

10—2

meaning and emotional tone of particular words and
sentences, but also of the structure and atmosphere
of the composition as a whole. This may be illustrated
by reference to Wordsworth's poem, *The Daffodils*: for
the sake of clearness, it will be well to quote the poem
in its entirety:

THE DAFFODILS.

I wandered lonely as a cloud   1
That floats on high o'er vales and hills,
When all at once I saw a crowd,
A host, of golden daffodils;
Beside the lake, beneath the trees,   5
Fluttering and dancing in the breeze.

Continuous as the stars that shine
And twinkle on the milky way,
They stretched in never-ending line
Along the margin of a bay: 10
Ten thousand saw I at a glance,
Tossing their heads in sprightly dance.

The waves beside them danced; but they
Outdid the sparkling waves in glee:
A poet could not but be gay,   15
In such a jocund company:
I gazed—and gazed—but little thought
What wealth the show to me had brought:

For oft, when on my couch I lie
In vacant or in pensive mood,   20
They flashed upon that inward eye
Which is the bliss of solitude;
And then my heart with pleasure fills,
And dances with the daffodils.

From the point of view of structure, this poem may
be divided into two parts: (1) lls. 1–18; (2) lls. 19–24.
Lines 1 to 16 are light and lively in tone: they

convey a sense of moving light and colour. The keynote is struck in such phrases as "fluttering and dancing in the breeze," "tossing their heads in sprightly dance." The lines should be read brightly and rather quickly, in the middle pitch, varied in some of the phrases according to the meaning. Lines 17 and 18 suggest a change of mood : they form the conclusion of the first part, and at the same time the prelude to the second part, of the poem. The significance of those lines may be brought out by prolonging the *ay* sound in "gazed" and by a slower delivery throughout.

The predominant tone of the second part is more reflective, and the change may be suggested by reading lls. 19 to 22 in a lower pitch and rather slowly and quietly. The concluding two lines, however, lls. 23 and 24, sound again the note of brightness and happiness characteristic of the poem as a whole, and in the reading of those the pace may be again quickened and the voice raised in pitch and loudness.

We may now consider more precisely how a passage in literature should be studied with a view to the expressive reading of it aloud. The following may be suggested as some of the chief points to which we should direct our attention :

1. What is the main idea, or the general meaning, of the passage ?

2. What is the general feeling or tone suggested ? By what adjective or adjectives may it be suitably described ?

3. How should the passage be read, so as to express its essential meaning and emotion, (*a*) in respect of the dominant pitch of the voice, (*b*) in respect of intensity

of voice—*i.e.*, loudness or softness, (*c*) in respect of the pace of utterance, quick or slow ?

4. Is the feeling or tone of the passage uniform throughout, or are there transitions and varying phases of feeling ? If there are, how may those transitions and phases be appropriately expressed by (*a*) variations of pitch, (*b*) degrees of loudness or softness, (*c*) variations of pace ?

5. What words or clauses or sentences should be emphasised by pauses or by varying stress ?

6. What is the general character of the vowel-sounds in the passage ? Does assonance occur ?

7. What is the general character of the consonant-sounds ? Is there any marked repetition of one or several consonant-sounds ? Are particular consonant-sounds used to produce particular mental effects ? Does alliteration, or onomatopoeia, occur ?

Those questions we may ask not only of ourselves before we read aloud, but also, at our discretion, of our pupils after we have read and before they are called upon to read a particular passage. It will be understood, of course, that the procedure here suggested is not meant to be followed in a hard-and-fast way: while it has been thought better, for the sake of clearness, to describe somewhat formally, and in considerable detail, the methods indicated throughout this book, the extent to which they are applicable, and the precise mode of their application, must vary in each case with the circumstances. Bearing in mind this proviso, let us examine a few particular passages in the light of the preceding remarks, and ask ourselves how they might be studied by the teacher, and treated in class, with a view to securing the expressive reading and a right appreciation of them by the pupils.

1. BLOW, BUGLE, BLOW.

The splendour falls on castle walls   1
    And snowy summits old in story;
The long light shakes across the lakes,
    And the wild cataract leaps in glory.
Blow, bugle, blow, set the wild echoes flying,   5
Blow, bugle; answer, echoes, dying, dying, dying.

    O hark, O hear! how thin and clear,
        And thinner, clearer, farther going!
    O sweet and far from cliff and scar
        The horns of Elfland faintly blowing!   10
    Blow, let us hear the purple glens replying:
    Blow, bugle; answer, echoes, dying, dying, dying.

    O love, they die in yon rich sky,
        They faint on hill or field or river:
    Our echoes roll from soul to soul,   15
        And grow for ever and for ever.
Blow, bugle, blow, set the wild echoes flying,
And answer, echoes, answer, dying, dying, dying.
                            TENNYSON.

The teacher may first read the poem to the class, expressing in his reading the results of his own previous study of the stanzas.

The pupils might then be asked to state the subject-matter in a few words. The poem is a descriptive lyric: it describes a situation, suggestively rather than explicitly. The situation is that of two lovers gazing at a picturesque landscape and listening to the sounds of a bugle and the gradually fading echoes. What time of day is indicated? There is no explicit indication of time, but the references to "the long light," "yon rich sky," and the whole tone of the poem, suggest "sunset and evening calm." Does any marked alteration of tone occur in the course of the poem ? In the last stanza a note of more personal feeling is struck : the sounds of the bugle faint and die, but the echoes that "roll from soul to soul" will "grow for ever." This change of tone must be expressed in the reading by an appropriate change in pitch, intensity, and pace. What lines are repeated, with slight variations, in each stanza ? What is the purpose of the refrain ? How should it be read ? Its first phrases are suggestive of the clear, ringing notes of the bugle and their loud first echoes : they should be spoken, therefore, in a higher pitch and more loudly than the lines that precede. The last phrases of the refrain express the gradual fading of the echoes, and to produce this effect the successive repetitions of the word "dying" should be marked by a gradual lowering of pitch and decrease in loudness.

The first two lines of the poem suggest the calmness and splendour of sunset. They might be read in fairly level tones, and on a medium pitch, while full value should be given to the long vowels. Line 3 is suggestive of a continuous chain of movement, line 4 of sudden movement. How may we render the characteristic effect of the third line ? By dwelling on the vowel-sounds, and especially on the o in "long," and by gradually and evenly raising the pitch of the voice on the word "long." In the fourth line "cataract" is onomatopoeic, and there should be a sudden rise in pitch on "leaps." Alliteration occurs in "snowy summits," "long light," and the repetition of l and r throughout the stanza produces a distinctly musical effect.

In the second stanza the reader must imagine that he hears—or rather, perhaps, he must actually hear—

the thin clear echoes sounding from cliff and scar and fading in the distance. The stanza should be read softly. In line 7 "hark" should be uttered with a rising intonation, and "hear" with a falling intonation. Notice the appropriately " thin " quality of the vowel-sounds in "thin," "clear," "thinner," "clearer," and their characteristic effect, contrasting with the long a and o in " farther " and " going."

In the third stanza, as we have remarked above, a note of deeper and more personal feeling is sounded. Lines 15 and 16 should be read on a higher pitch, and with a growing intensity of voice and feeling. "Our" in line 15 may be emphasised, and a pause for effect may be made after the first "for ever" in line 16. Assonance occurs in "Our echoes roll from soul to soul." The long o's are expressive, and the r sound is used in those lines with characteristic effect.

2. HE FELL AMONG THIEVES.

" Ye have robb'd," said he, "ye have slaughter'd and made an end,
  Take your ill-got plunder, and bury the dead:
What will ye more of your guest and sometime friend?"
  "Blood for our blood," they said.

He laugh'd: "If one may settle the score for five,   5
  I am ready; but let the reckoning stand till day:
I have loved the sunlight as dearly as any alive."
  "You shall die at dawn," said they.

He flung his empty revolver down the slope,
  He climb'd alone to the Eastward edge of the trees;   10
All night long in a dream untroubled of hope
  He brooded, clasping his knees.

He did not hear the monotonous roar that fills
  The ravine where the Yassîn river sullenly flows;
He did not see the starlight on the Laspur hills,   15
  Or the far Afghan snows.

He saw the April noon on his books aglow,
　The wistaria trailing in at the window wide;
He heard his father's voice from the terrace below
　Calling him down to ride.　　　　　　　　　　　20

He saw the gray little church across the park,
　The mounds that hid the loved and honour'd dead;
The Norman arch, the chancel softly dark,
　The brasses black and red.

He saw the School Close, sunny and green,　　　　25
　The runner beside him, the stand by the parapet wall,
The distant tape, and the crowd roaring between,
　His own name over all.

He saw the dark wainscot and timber'd roof,
　The long tables, and the faces merry and keen;　30
The College Eight and their trainer dining aloof,
　The Dons on the daïs serene.

He watch'd the liner's stem ploughing the foam,
　He felt her trembling speed and the thrash of her screw;
He heard her passengers' voices talking of home,　35
　He saw the flag she flew.

And now it was dawn. He rose strong on his feet,
　And strode to his ruin'd camp below the wood;
He drank the breath of the morning cool and sweet;
　His murderers round him stood.　　　　　　　40

Light on the Laspur hills was broadening fast,
　The blood-red snow-peaks chill'd to a dazzling white;
He turn'd, and saw the golden circle at last,
　Cut by the Eastern height.

"O glorious Life, Who dwellest in earth and sun,　45
　I have lived, I praise and adore Thee."
　　　　　　　　　　A sword swept.
Over the pass the voices one by one
　Faded, and the hill slept.　　　　　　　NEWBOLT.

Having read the poem to the pupils, the teacher
might call on them to state briefly the subject-matter.
He might then ask: Into what parts or sections may

the subject-matter naturally be divided ? Lines 1 to 8 may be taken as forming the first part : they contain the elements of narrative and present a dramatic situation in conversational form. The second part, lines 9 to 36, describes the Englishman's visions and thoughts through the night, and is introspective in character. The third division, lines 37 to 48, resuming the narrative strain, tells the tragic conclusion. How, in our reading, are we to express the subject-matter of those successive phases and their characteristic tone ?

The poem opens with a few staccato phrases, suggestive of the hero's outspoken courage : in the first three lines, therefore, an emphatic style of delivery should be adopted. The tribesmen's grim reply in the fourth line might then be read more slowly and on a lower pitch. In reading the first two lines of the second stanza the pitch would be raised again. The leading *motif* of the poem is sounded for the first time in the seventh line : "I have loved the sunlight as dearly as any alive." How is its significance to be brought out ? In the first place, perhaps, by a slight pause at the beginning of the line, secondly, by lowering the pitch and intensity of the voice, and, thirdly, by reading the line more slowly and in a significant and reflective tone. In the eighth line the phrase, "you shall die at dawn," sounds a theme that is repeated and elaborated in the last section and is important for the proper understanding and appreciation of the poem—the words "at dawn" might be slightly emphasised. Throughout the section, and, indeed, the whole poem, the repetition of the nasal consonants m, n, and ng add to the sonority of the lines, and r and l are also frequently used.

The first eight lines of the second section (9—16) may be read in an ordinary narrative tone. They form a prelude to the main part of the section, contained in lines 17 to 36, which describe the Englishman's visions and dreams : in reading these lines the voice should be lowered, and the intonation—more or less " level " in character—should convey to the hearers that what the hero sees is seen only in dream.

The transition to the third section, at line 37, is marked by a short, arresting phrase of monosyllabic words, recalling the theme of the last line in the first section. The tribesmen had promised their victim a respite through the night; " and now—it was dawn." The words should be spoken significantly, and the contrast between the darkness and dreams of night and the light and life of morning may be conveyed by a rise in pitch and loudness. The vigour of manhood, the beauty and glory of life, the splendour of the sun, and the hero's dauntless faith in the triumph of life over death, are the themes that follow. In lines 37 and 38 the significant use of the monosyllables, long vowels, r's, and the resonant n, ng, and m should be noted. The section should be read with a gradually increasing intensity of feeling, culminating in lines 45 and 46, which concentrate in a few triumphant and final phrases the main *motif*—

> O glorious Life, Who dwellest in earth and sun,
> I have lived, I praise and adore Thee.

The close of the poem is quiet but dramatic. The change of tone is marked by a significant and arresting phrase of three monosyllables, " A sword swept." A pause should be made before and after those words, and they might be spoken slowly and on a lower pitch. The phrases that follow in the two concluding lines, suggestive of rest and peace, fade away to a quiet music, depending for its effect mainly on the repetition of the s sound and on the musical sequence of the consonants p v b f.

3. PASSAGE FROM BURKE'S "SPEECH ON CONCILIATION WITH AMERICA."

As loNg as you have the wisdoM to keep the sovereigN authority of this couNtry as the saNctuary of liberty, the sacred teMple consecrated to our coMMon faith, wherever the choseN race and soNs of ENglaNd worship freedoM, they will turN their faces toward you. The More they Multiply, the More frieNds you will have; the More ardeNtly they love liberty, the More perfect will be their obedieNce. Slavery they caN have aNywhere. It is a weed that grows in every soil. They May have it froM SpaiN; they May have it froM Prussia; but, uNtil you becoMe lost to all feeliNG of your true iNterest and your Natural digNity, freedoM they caN have froM NoNe but you. This is the coM- Modity of price, of which you have the MoNopoly. This is the true Act of NavigatioN, which biNds to you the coMMerce of the coloNies, and through theM secures to you the wealth of the world....

All this, I kNow well eNough, will souNd wild and chiMerical to the profaNe herd of those vulgar and MechaNical politiciaNs, who have No place amoNG us; a sort of people who thiNk that NothiNG exists but what is gross and Material, and who, therefore, far froM beiNG qualified to be directors of the great MoveMeNt of eMpire, are Not fit to turN a wheel iN the MachiNe. But to MeN truly iNitiated and rightly taught, these ruliNG and Master principles, which, iN the opiNioN of such MeN as I have MeNtioNed, have No substaNtial existeNce, are in truth everythiNG and all iN all. MagNaNiMity iN politics is Not seldoM the truest wisdoM; and a great eMpire and little MiNds go ill together. If we are coNscious of our statioN, and glow with zeal to fill our places as becoMes our situatioN and ourselves, we ought to auspicate all our public proceediNGs on AMerica with the old warNiNG of the church, *sursuM corda*! We ought to elevate our MiNds to the greatNess of that trust to which the order of ProvideNce has called us. By advertiNG to the digNity of this high calliNG, our aNcestors have turNed a savage wilderNess into a glorious eMpire, and have Made the Most exteNsive, and the oNly hoNourable coNquests, Not by destroyiNG, but by proMotiNG, the wealth, the NuMber, the happiNess, of the huMaN race. Let us get aN AMericaN reveNue as we have got aN AMericaN eMpire. ENglish privileges have Made it all that it is; ENglish privileges aloNe will Make it all it caN be.

The passage is one of sustained and lofty eloquence, in the periodic style, and should be delivered with vigour and earnestness. The first paragraph contains an emphatic assertion of the principle of conciliation and liberty: "freedom they can have from none but you : this is the commodity of price of which you have the monopoly." In the second paragraph the speaker asserts that the policy of conciliation is advisable not only from the higher standpoint of morality and religion but also from that of expediency : " magnanimity in politics is not seldom the truest wisdom ; and a great empire and little minds go ill together."

Three phases may be distinguished in the exposition of the first paragraph :

(1) Sentences 1—3, down to the phrase, " the more perfect will be their obedience " ;

(2) from " slavery they can have anywhere" to " they may have it from Prussia " ;

(3) from " but until you become lost " to " secures to you the wealth of the world."

The main theme of the first and third phases is sounded in the word " freedom " ; and they are separated from one another by a contrasted phase of which the theme is " slavery." The subject-matter, therefore, indicates that the delivery of the first and third sections of the paragraph should be marked by a general similarity of pitch, loudness, and emotional tone ; while in the second section there should be some modification of the voice in those respects.

The opening words, down to "faith," might be spoken in sustained and fairly level tones, while the clauses that follow, down to " obedience," should be delivered in tones expressive of emphatic conviction. The contrasted theme of " slavery " is then introduced, and the pitch of the voice should be lowered, and the emotional tone should become less fervent. At the word " but " the pitch might again be raised, and the concluding sentences of the paragraph should be delivered energetically, the words " freedom " and " this " being significantly emphasised.

The wave of feeling momentarily subsides, and the

speaker alludes to "the profane herd of vulgar and mechanical politicians" who look upon his ideals as impracticable. The opening sentence of the second paragraph, down to "machine," might therefore be spoken on a lower pitch, with some restrained note of censure and disdain on the words " vulgar and mechanical politicians," " a sort of people," etc. At the words " But to men truly initiated " the main theme is resumed, and is elaborated with increasing energy and emotion to the end of the passage. The short concluding sentences, following several longer and more sustained periods, give a pointed and emphatic finish.

From a phonetic point of view, the most striking feature of the passage is the continuous repetition of the nasal consonants m, n, ng, which adds to the resonant effect characteristic of sustained eloquence. The r sound and the p b v f sequence also occur frequently. The rhythmical mingling of long and short sentences should be noticed. In the closing sentences the use of monosyllabic words, many of them ending with the sharp t sound, produces a significant effect.

Before concluding this chapter, a few words must be said on the reading and acting of Shakespeare in class. It is an encouraging circumstance that within the last few years the study of Shakespeare has become much more prevalent in our schools than at any previous time. The enthusiastic advocacy and testimony of such writers as Mr H. Caldwell Cook in *The Play Way* have done much to promote the acting of Shakespearean drama by pupils of school age.

" The best way to make a start in class-room acting," says Mr Cook, " is to take a play of Shakespeare and act it....However young the boys may be, provided they are over 10, a Shakespeare play is the most useful beginning [1]." With this dictum we may all agree; but, while agreeing, we should be careful to form a just notion of the value of such acting for junior pupils, and of the limitations to its value. It may be considered that Mr Cook's enthusiasm, while it constitutes the supreme merit of the book from which we have quoted, is apt to lead him to overlook some of the limitations that must necessarily attach to the reading and study of Shakespeare by pupils below the age of 14.

The desire to " act a part " appears in children at a very early age, and in their daily play they derive much pleasure from representing themselves as soldiers, sailors, shopkeepers, the mothers of families, etc.; the assumption of a grown-up character satisfies their self-regarding instinct and stimulates the feeling of superiority, a craving for which is as strongly marked in children as in those of more mature years. This characteristic of our pupils should be turned to use in the class-room : it forms the fundamental justification of the method that Mr Cook terms " the play way."

In the reading of Shakespeare, then, it is the teacher's business to utilise the play-instinct of the pupils to the best advantage, and to arrange that the reading should be done under the most favourable conditions possible. Although greatly improved methods are now employed generally in the reading of Shakespeare, teachers still too often adopt the practice of simply calling upon the pupils to read in succession

[1] *The Play Way: an Essay in Educational Method.* By H. Caldwell Cook, M.A. London : William Heinemann, 1917.

from their seats in the class-room. This should *never* be done. A better plan is to bring the pupils out to play their parts in front of the class; they should then be expected not only to read but also to accompany the words with appropriate gesture and action : as Mr Cook remarks, "to ignore action is to ignore the play, and a book in the hand is not a very serious impediment to a boy who has the chance to stab some one, or to storm a city wall."

Most class-rooms, however, it must be admitted, do not provide a suitable environment for play-acting. As a rule, the space available in front of the class is too limited. The school hall, which is generally empty during the greater part of the day, should be utilised, as a matter of course, whenever pupils are called upon to act Shakespeare. If a platform is available, we may approximate the conditions of the presentation the more nearly to those of the Shakespearean stage. A line should be marked out on the floor to represent the limits of the inner and outer stages, and a table or a blackboard may be used as substitutes for the balcony and upper windows.

For pupils between the ages of 10 and 14 the treatment of Shakespearean drama should consist mainly in the reading and acting of the plays. Believing that much may be gained by junior pupils from the study of Shakespeare on suitable lines, we shall yet do well to recognise that they are capable of appreciating only certain aspects of the plays. They can understand and enjoy the incidents, and especially the more sensational elements, of the plot—the fights, the pageantry, the "alarums and excursions," the life and movement and action of the shifting scenes; and they can appreciate also the broad and graphic delineation of character. And those are precisely the elements that they may be best enabled to appreciate and enjoy through the acting of the plays. But pupils of this age are as yet not capable of appreciating truly the essential nature of drama and dramatic effect; so that the serious study of drama as drama must be regarded as belonging to a later period. In a previous chapter we have stated some of the reasons, inherent in the nature of drama, why this should be so, and dealt with drama generally as a subject of more serious study for pupils over the age of 14. It may be added that for senior pupils, while the expressive reading of Shakespeare should form an essential part of their class-work, the acting of the plays in class is not so feasible. Pupils over 14 are more self-conscious and more critical, to such an extent as to make difficult and undesirable, if not impossible, the acting of a play in the somewhat crude style alone possible in the course of ordinary class-work. But the representation of the plays in the junior classes, by gesture and action as well as by reading, forms an excellent preparation for the more developed reading and more advanced studies of the senior classes.

CHAPTER XI.

SUGGESTIONS FOR A COURSE OF STUDY, WITH SPECIAL REFERENCE TO ADVANCED COURSES.

WHEN we seek to formulate a course of study in any subject, the first step we may take is to distinguish, broadly, between the successive stages into which the course may appropriately be divided. In the remarks that follow four stages are discriminated, according to the ages of the pupils concerned: Stage I, for pupils up to the age of eleven; Stage II, for pupils between eleven and fourteen; Stage III, for pupils from fourteen to sixteen; and Stage IV, for pupils over sixteen[1]. It will be understood, of course, that those stages are not mutually exclusive, but interfuse.

In arranging the work of the various stages it will be helpful to keep in view a few general principles.

The first, and perhaps the most important of those may be termed the Principle of Variety and Interest, which indicates that, with a view to stimulating and maintaining interest, the work set at each stage should be as wide and varied as possible. One of the main

---

[1] This classification of stages corresponds with that adopted in an excellent pamphlet, which all teachers of English should see, written by Members of the English Association, entitled *The Essentials of English Teaching* (Longmans, Green, and Co., 1919), to which I have been indebted for various suggestions in the writing of this chapter.

reasons for the defectiveness of English Literature teaching in the past was that the curriculum was much too narrow : often a whole year was spent in the reading of only one or two books. It is now recognised that a wider and more varied course of reading is desirable ; and we should remember, too, that the course may be made more interesting if we arrange skilfully the succession of the books selected for study—for instance, the reading of poetry may be followed by the reading of prose, and after literature that is bright and lively or exciting in tone something more serious and of a slower movement may be read.

If we aim thus at making the course of reading as wide and varied as possible, the teacher's method of treatment must necessarily be more general and less detailed. But, at the same time, his treatment of the subject-matter must not be superficial : in deciding the number and character of the books to be studied at each stage, we should be guided not only by the Principle of Variety and Interest, but also by the Principle of Thoroughness. As a rule, the older the pupils are, the more time should be devoted to detailed study; but even in Stage I, short poems and prose passages may, from time to time, be treated more intensively ; and, after Stage I, in each half-year a text suitable for detailed study should be included in the course, while other books may be read more rapidly.

A third principle that should be considered is the Principle of Correlation. Regarded as subjects in the school curriculum, Literature has obvious natural affinities with Composition and History, and it is desirable that we should take those into account in framing the course in Literature.

The chief literary forms—fiction, the essay, narrative and epic poetry, the lyric, etc.—contain in varying degrees, separately or intermingled, the elements of narration, description, exposition, and discussion or argument—the main types of literary composition. And just as, in the study of composition, our pupils should be taught to write simple narratives and descriptions before they attempt the expository or the argumentative style, so for the earlier stages in the study of literature books should be selected that are mainly narrative and descriptive in character, while the study of forms in which exposition or argument is predominant (*e.g.*, the oration) should be reserved for later stages. Through such an arrangement the teaching of literature may proceed hand in hand with the teaching of composition. But it should be remembered that at no stage should the pupils' reading be narrowly confined to one literary form, and that, indeed, it is impossible to draw any absolute distinction between the various forms in respect of their elements, since, for example, most fiction is not purely narrative, but contains the elements of description, and frequently of exposition and argument, while narrative poetry, also, may be at the same time descriptive, and sometimes even expository, in its style.

The study of history, too, is closely related to the study of literature. Many literary works reflect accurately the character of the times when they were produced, and are, in part, the product of historical influences and movements. But, while it is true to say that a knowledge of the history of a period is necessary to the thorough understanding of its literature, and that literature, in its turn, illustrates the social and political environment, it may be held that this consideration should not exercise any appreciable influence on the course of reading set for younger pupils, whose interests and knowledge are not sufficiently wide to enable them to understand the relation between the literary production and the history of a period. In the scheme outlined below it is recommended that no systematic attempt to correlate the study of literature with that of history should be made until the fourth stage of the course has been reached.

The preceding remarks lead naturally to the consideration of a fourth principle, the Principle of Chronology. In planning our scheme we should ask ourselves: How far is it desirable that the books included in the course should be read in chronological order, according to the date of their production, with a view to imparting to our pupils some connected knowledge of the development of English Literature ? Most teachers will agree in thinking that it would be highly undesirable to arrange the course throughout on chronological lines, and that at the earlier stages our choice of books should be determined exclusively by their subject-matter and style and atmosphere, by their inherent suitability to the age and attainments of the class. To limit our choice of books throughout with respect to the Principle of Chronology would be to submit ourselves unduly to the narrowing influence of an academic ideal, and would interfere seriously with the possibility of realising the true aims of literary teaching. The systematic study of the development of English Literature may well be deferred to the fourth stage of the course, though it may be possible to give the pupils some more informal ideas on the subject in earlier stages—for instance, if even a junior class should be reading a selection of lyric poems or prose passages, the pupils' attention might be drawn informally to the manner in which the selections illustrate the development of our literature.

At this point, before we proceed to define specifically the work of the various stages, it will be well to remark that the suggestions offered in this chapter are merely tentative : dogmatically and authoritatively to propound a fixed course of study would be absurd, for what might be suitable, or possible to realise, in one school might be wholly or partially unsuitable, or impossible of realisation, in another, and, again, in the selection of particular books the teacher's personal tastes ought always to be given due weight. The books referred to in the following paragraphs have been chosen as being, in the writer's opinion, suitable for the stage in connection with which they are mentioned, but many others would, no doubt, be equally or more suitable. Again, the amount of time devoted to English literature may vary in different schools. The writer does not imagine that pupils would have time to study all the books he has mentioned in connection with each stage, and this remark applies especially to the later stages of the course, in describing which it has been thought well to err in the direction of over-fulness rather than of paucity of suggestion, since the greater the number of suggestions offered the greater is the probability that some at least may meet with the reader's approval.

In accordance with the principles to which we have referred above, during the first stage of the course (for pupils up to the age of eleven) the literature read should be narrative and descriptive in style, and (as at all stages) the relation between the teaching of literature and the teaching of composition should be kept in view.

The old Classical and Norse legends and myths, as represented in such books as Hawthorne's *Stories of Ancient Greece*, Lamb's *Adventures of Ulysses*, and Keary's *Heroes of Asgard*, with the Fairy Tales of Andersen, Grimm, and *The Arabian Nights*, form suitable reading at this stage; and of modern prose fiction written more specifically for children a selection may be made from Defoe's *Robinson Crusoe*, Irving's *Rip Van Winkle* and *The Legend of Sleepy Hollow*, Kingsley's *Water Babies*, Lewis Carroll's *Alice in Wonderland*, Dickens's *Christmas Carol* and *The Cricket on the Hearth*, Ruskin's *King of the Golden River*, Stevenson's *Treasure Island*, Kipling's *Jungle Book*, *Puck of Pook's Hill*, and *Rewards and Fairies*, etc.

At this stage, too, the study of lyric poetry should be begun, in its simpler forms, as represented in the poems of Blake, Stevenson (*e.g.*, "The Land of Story Books," "My Shadow," "My Ship and I"), George Macdonald ("The Wind and the Moon"), Arnold ("The Forsaken Merman"), William Allingham ("The Fairies"), Mary Lamb, and others.

A selection of the early ballads and of short narrative poems like "The Wreck of the Hesperus," "Lord Ullin's Daughter," "The Loss of the Royal George," "John Gilpin," "The Burial of Sir John Moore," should also be included[1]; and some longer poems should be read (*e.g.*, *Hiawatha, Tales of a Wayside Inn, Goblin Market, The Pied Piper*).

[1] cf. sup. pp. 89—94.

In the second stage (for pupils from eleven to fourteen) the teaching may proceed on similar lines, the literature chosen being mainly narrative and descriptive. But throughout this stage an important place should be given to the reading and acting of Shakespeare's plays, on the lines suggested in Chapter X[1]; a selection may be made from *A Midsummer Night's Dream, As You Like It, Twelfth Night, The Merchant of Venice, King John, Richard III, Henry V, Julius Caesar.*

The study of lyric poetry should be continued, and the lyrics read may be longer and more difficult than at the first stage.

In romantic narrative poetry Scott's poems should be given chief place [2], and Coleridge's *Ancient Mariner*, Arnold's *Sohrab and Rustum*, and Tennyson's *Idylls of the King* may also be read. Examples of more realistic narrative poetry appropriate to this stage are *The Deserted Village, Evangeline,* and *Enoch Arden.*

Prose narrative may be represented by *The Vicar of Wakefield*, the novels of Scott and Dickens, *Silas Marner*, Reade's *Cloister and the Hearth*, Kingsley's *Westward Ho*, Stevenson's *Black Arrow, Kidnapped, Catriona*, etc.

During the later part of this stage more attention should be given to literature in which the descriptive element is stronger, as, for instance, in prose : Borrow's *Lavengro* and *The Bible in Spain*, Anne Manning's *Household of Sir Thomas More*, Jefferies's *Wild Life in a Southern Country*, Stevenson's *Travels with a Donkey* and *Inland Voyage*; or, in poetry : the *Elegy in a Country Churchyard, The Traveller*, Shelley's *The Cloud* and *The Skylark*, and parts of *Childe Harold*.

[1] v. pp. 160—163.   [2] cf. sup. pp. 99—103.

In the third stage (for pupils between fourteen and sixteen) the range of the prose and poetry read should be still further extended, and the teaching may become more thorough and systematic.

Shakespeare's plays should now be studied more intensively, and it might be advisable to limit our choice to those belonging to the first two periods of his development, reserving those of the two later periods for the next stage of the course. To Shakespeare's first period belong *A Midsummer Night's Dream*, *Love's Labour's Lost*, *The Two Gentlemen of Verona*, *Romeo and Juliet*; and to his second *As You Like It*, *The Merchant of Venice*, *Twelfth Night*, *Much Ado about Nothing*, *King John*, *Julius Caesar*, *Henry V*: from each of those periods we may select for detailed treatment one or more plays not previously read.

Narrative and descriptive poetry, the lyric, letters (*e.g.*, selections from Cowper, Gray, Lamb, FitzGerald, etc.), and historical and biographical prose may also be represented, and in fiction the pupils may read some of the works of later and contemporary writers (*e.g.*, Bulwer Lytton: *The Last Days of Pompeii*, *The Last of the Barons*. George Eliot: *The Mill on the Floss*. Thackeray: *Esmond*, *Pendennis*. Hardy: *The Trumpet Major*, *Far from the Madding Crowd*. Blackmore: *Lorna Doone*).

At this stage an advance should be made to the more detailed study of exposition in literature. A selection of essays varying in subject-matter and style should be studied on the lines suggested in Chapter IV, due attention being given to the correlation of literature and composition.

After the age of fifteen the study of argument may

be begun, on the lines indicated in Chapter VIII, a suitable selection of speeches being used for this purpose.

In the fourth stage (for pupils over 16) a more systematic study of the development of English Literature should be attempted, and a short connected History of English Literature may be used as a text-book, for reference if not for continuous reading. A scholarly book of selected passages in prose and verse, arranged chronologically, of the kind described in the quotation from Miss Elizabeth Lee on page 38 above, may be considered to form the most convenient medium for the study of the characteristics of successive authors and periods.

An important point to bear in mind at this stage is that, as far as possible, the pupils should derive their ideas as to the development of our literature directly from the reading of the authors. Besides using a suitable book of selections, they should study, more or less intensively, some of the works of the most representative authors of successive periods.

The detailed study of Shakespeare will be continued, and the plays chosen may be some of those that illustrate the third and fourth periods of his development, as *Hamlet, Macbeth, King Lear, Othello, Antony and Cleopatra,* for the third period, and *The Winter's Tale, Cymbeline,* and *The Tempest,* for the fourth.

Chaucer's *Canterbury Tales,* Spenser's *Faerie Queene,* and Milton's *Paradise Lost* [1] belong appropriately to this stage of the course; and Dryden (*Absalom and Achitophel,* Part I), Pope (*The Rape of the Lock*), Cowper

[1] v. sup. pp. 96—99.

(*The Task*, Book IV), Wordsworth (Matthew Arnold's Golden Treasury Selection), Byron (*Childe Harold*), and Tennyson (*In Memoriam*) may all be regarded as representative of their periods.

In prose there might be read : Sir Thomas Browne (*Religio Medici* or *Urn-Burial*), Swift (*The Battle of the Books*), Johnson (*Lives of the Poets*), Burke (on Conciliation with America), Landor, Ruskin, Carlyle.

Time would not permit of the intensive study of all the works or writers we have mentioned, and, in the case of some, the book of selections would provide sufficient material for study.

It may be recommended, too, that at this stage the development of our literature should be followed right up to recent and contemporary literature. In this connexion the reading of an " up-to-date " novel (*e.g.*, Wells's *Mr Britling*) may be made particularly suggestive, as illustrating the elasticity of form of which the novel is capable, many of the novels of to-day being no longer confined to the narrative and descriptive style, but containing also, in a marked degree, the elements of exposition and argument. The reading of a modern play (*e.g.*, Galsworthy's *The Silver Box*) may be made equally suggestive.

The Board of Education Regulations for Secondary Schools now recognise English as one of the subjects that may be included in the " Advanced Courses " of " Modern Studies[1]."

So far as English Literature is concerned, the work of such an "Advanced Course" may have a twofold aim.

---

[1] v. Board of Education Regulations for Secondary Schools, England, 1919, Chapter VIII, p. 18.

In the first place, the pupils should gain a general knowledge of the development of our literature as a whole, through the first-hand reading of the works, or selections from the works, of representative authors, this part of the course being conducted on similar lines to those that have just been described as appropriate to the ordinary course for pupils over sixteen.

And, secondly, the pupils in the "Advanced Course" should gain a more detailed knowledge of a particular period or of a particular phase of literary production during a period; and this specialised and intensive study should constitute the characteristic and chief feature of the Course. The works of the most important and attractive writers of the period or literary phase under consideration should be studied, some of them rapidly and others intensively, some, again, only partially, and others as wholes.

The following outline may be suggested for such a course of study on "Shakespeare and his Predecessors and Contemporaries":

1. For general reading, *The Chester Pageant of the Deluge*, and *Everyman*[1].

These might be read as representing the early miracle and morality plays, which are highly interesting as being among the few authentic examples in English Literature of a thoroughly democratic and communistic form of art. The chief reason, however, for including a miracle play and a morality in this course of reading is that those forms represent an early stage in the history

---

[1] v. *Everyman, with other Interludes, including Eight Miracle Plays* (J. M. Dent and Sons: Everyman's Library).

of the drama[1]. Their relation to later drama may be compared in some respects with that of the early ballads to later narrative poetry.

2. For general reading, selected passages from *Ralph Roister Doister* and *Gorboduc,* as representing early comedy and tragedy.

3. Shakespeare's predecessors :

For general reading :

 Greene : *Friar Bacon and Friar Bungay.*

 Kyd : *The Spanish Tragedy.*

For intensive study :

 Marlowe : *Faustus.*

4. For intensive study :

Shakespeare : one or two plays from each of the four periods of his development as a dramatist.

In a course of this kind it is important that the pupils should compare carefully for themselves the plays of the successive periods with reference to their plot, characterization, style, metre, and mood or tendency of thought. For instance, if the pupils had read *A Midsummer Night's Dream, Henry V, Hamlet,* and *The Tempest,* such questions as the following might be suggested for their consideration : What differences do you notice between *A Midsummer Night's Dream* and *Henry V* in respect of management of plot, characterization, and style ? How had Shakespeare developed since writing the earlier play ? Contrast the characters of Henry V and Hamlet. How does the Shakespeare who wrote *Hamlet* differ from the Shakespeare who wrote

---

[1] Most of the best authorities (*e.g.*, **Ward, Saintsbury, Courthope**) agree in thinking that our modern drama arose out of the miracle plays, though this is sometimes disputed.

Henry V? Can this difference be explained by reference
to Shakespeare's life ? What passages would you select
from *A Midsummer Night's Dream* and from *The Tempest*
to illustrate the difference in style between the two
plays ? What passages would you select from *Hamlet*
and from *The Tempest* to illustrate clearly the different
moods in which the two plays were written ?

5. Shakespeare's contemporaries :

For general reading :

Jonson : *The Alchemist.*

Beaumont and Fletcher: *The Knight of the Burn-
ing Pestle.*

Webster: *The Duchess of Malfi.*

The following, again, may be cited as an outline
of the special study of a period—that of Caroline
Literature, or, as it may suitably be described, Cavalier
and Puritan Literature :

1. For intensive study :

Milton : *Paradise Lost,* I to IV.

For general reading :

Paradise Lost, V to XII.

2. For general reading :

Selections from Crashaw, Herbert, and Vaughan.

Selections from Suckling, Lovelace, and Marvell.

Selections from Herrick's *Hesperides,* including
Noble Numbers.

The poetry of some of those Cavalier writers, such
as Suckling, Lovelace, and Herrick, is precisely of the
kind that may most appropriately follow the study of
Milton. After some time spent in the study of Milton
our pupils may turn to the lighter numbers of those
poets with a natural feeling of relief. Such a feeling

many of us must have experienced in the course of our reading. Sir William Watson gives fine expression to it in his recently published volume when he says:

> So have I turned, when overbrooded long
> By that great star-familiar peak austere,
> My Milton's Sinai—Helicon divine,
> To some far earthlier singer's earth-sweet song:
> A song frail as the windflower, and as dear,
> With no more purpose than the eglantine[1].

3. For general reading:
Passages from Milton's *Areopagitica*.
Passages from Jeremy Taylor's *Holy Dying*.
Walton: *The Compleat Angler, Life of George Herbert.*

For detailed study:
Sir Thomas Browne: *Religio Medici.*
Bunyan: *The Pilgrim's Progress.*

In the course of this general reading and intensive study of authors, the pupils' attention should be explicitly directed to the main literary characteristics and tendencies of the period under consideration. Thus, in dealing with Cavalier and Puritan Literature, it would be shown (by reference more particularly to Crashaw and Vaughan) that much of the poetry of the period was marked by a certain strangeness and unnaturalness of expression, and that this over-subtlety and obscurity of the "metaphysical" poets produced later, by a natural reaction, the "correct" school of Dryden and Pope. In prose writing, again, it would be pointed out that one of the chief characteristics of the

---

[1] *The Superhuman Antagonists, and other Poems.* By Sir William Watson. Hodder and Stoughton.

period is the frequent occurrence of long and involved sentences formed in imitation of classical models (*cf.*, for instance, the prose of Milton, Jeremy Taylor, Sir Thomas Browne), and that just as the obscurity of the metaphysical school led, by reaction, to the clearness and correctness of Pope and his followers, so too the complicated syntax of Milton and Taylor and Browne was succeeded by the simple and elegant style of Addison and Steele.

Characteristic features in the subject-matter of the literature of the period under consideration would also be noticed. For instance, in the study of Cavalier and Puritan Literature, the pupils' attention would be drawn to the frequency with which the moral and religious note is sounded by the writers of the period. This characteristic may be accounted for largely by historical reasons. The early part of the period was a time of civil war, when grave and vital issues were at stake, and it was natural that the seriousness of the time should be reflected in its literature. Another characteristic of the poetry of this period is the frequent occurrence of panegyrics on individual persons (*cf.*, Milton's *Lycidas*, etc.), and this also may be explained partly on historical grounds. Protestantism, and more particularly Puritanism, tended always to exalt the claims of the individual, while a time of conflict is well fitted to bring into prominence individual leaders whose praises may be fitly sung in verse. It may be noted, however, that while the Puritan writers most often celebrated the valour and virtue of men, the Cavalier poets tended to idealise rather the beauty and graces of women.

We have here touched upon the relation between

the literature and the history of a period. In an "Advanced Course" the study of these should go together. The Board of Education Regulations prescribe, as one of the necessary elements in every "Advanced Course" of Modern Studies, a knowledge of English History. It may be suggested, then, that the period of English Literature selected for special study should be treated in detail also in the History class, the teachers of those subjects cooperating to their mutual advantage. The effective study of History by senior pupils involves some study of original documents, and among the most important of these are the books that we describe as "literature"; in particular, the social life and manners and customs of a period are reflected in its literature much more intimately and vividly than in the more arid and dreary contemporary documents from which the historian is wont to derive much of his material. On the other hand, as has been indicated in the preceding paragraph, we cannot properly understand the literature of a period apart from the consideration of its history. Often, indeed, to understand the literature of a period, we must know something of historical events that happened long before, and in other countries than our own, the study of English Literature and History being inextricably bound up with that of European Literature and History. For instance, in the course on "Shakespeare and his Predecessors and Contemporaries," or in any detailed course dealing with Elizabethan Literature, our pupils should be led to realize how the Italian Renaissance and the New Learning, the Reformation, and the progress of scientific and geographical discovery were all influences

favourable to freedom of thought and its expression in
art and literature; and how the break with the papacy,
the development of the navy, the voyages of Drake and
his compeers, and the struggle with Spain, intensified
the feeling of national importance and unity, and led to
its expression in literature in the passionate praise of
England and the Queen. In the course on Cavalier and
Puritan Literature, again, it would have to be pointed
out that under the early Stuart Kings the character of
most of the literature produced was widely different
from that written in the age of Elizabeth, and that the
adequate explanation of this fact involves a reference
to history. "No greater moral change," says J. R. Green,
"ever passed over a nation than passed over England
during the years which parted the middle of the reign
of Elizabeth from the meeting of the Long Parliament[1],"
and a corresponding change passed over the spirit of
literature. While most of the Elizabethan writers express the free spirit and widened interests of a period
of expansion and of heightened national consciousness, the
Cavalier and Puritan writers, on the other hand, generally
exhibit a more restrained and less joyous attitude towards life. They have lost, too, the uplifting sense of
national unity that had been characteristic of the
Elizabethans; as is remarked by Mr Stopford Brooke,
the strife in politics between the Divine Right of Kings
and Liberty, and in religion between the Church and
the Puritans, had grown "so defined and intense that
England ceased to be at one, and the poets (and prose-
writers) represented the parties, not the whole of
England."

[1] *A Short History of the English People*, Chap. VIII.

In the preceding paragraph we have sought to emphasize that the wider implications and relations of English Literature as a subject of study should be suggested to the pupils taking the Advanced Courses, and we have mentioned its relationship to history as an instance. Another aspect of the subject that the pupils should be led to consider is literary criticism and its development. The study of literary criticism may be begun with more particular reference to the most important author of the special period that may be under consideration—for instance, in the course on Shakespeare and his Predecessors, with reference to Shakespeare, and, in the course on Cavalier and Puritan Literature, with reference to Milton. The views of the chief critical writers who have dealt with Shakespeare's or with Milton's works, from the time of their production onwards, should be discussed, and the pupils will thus be enabled to form some idea of the changing attitudes of critical theory at different times. If possible, the pupils themselves should have access to the critical works to which reference is made. Thus some of the following might be consulted with regard to Shakespeare: Johnson, Preface to Edition of the Plays; Coleridge, *Lectures and Notes upon Shakespeare*; Hazlitt, *Characters of Shakespeare's Plays*; Dowden, *Shakespeare; his Mind and Art*; Bradley, *Shakespearean Tragedy*; Lee, *Life of Shakespeare*; or, with regard to Milton, some of the following: Addison, Essays in *The Spectator*; Macaulay, Essay on Milton; Arnold, *Essays in Criticism, Second Series*; Masson, *Life and Times of John Milton*; Dowden, *Puritan and Anglican: Studies in Literature*; Pattison, *Milton,* in "English Men of Letters" Series.

Our pupils' view of the subject should be widened also by the reading, in good translations, if not in the original language, of foreign works similar in kind to those written by the chief author of their period. Thus, along with Shakespeare's plays, one or two of the old Greek tragedies should be read[1]; or, by pupils taking French in their "Advanced Course," one or two of Racine's plays. The reading of *Paradise Lost*, again, should be accompanied or followed by the reading of a portion, at least, of the *Iliad*, the *Odyssey*, or the *Æneid*. A comparative study of works belonging to the same form of literature, but written by authors of different nationalities and periods, would lead naturally to a discussion of the characteristic qualities of that form—as of the drama in the case of Shakespeare and Sophocles and Racine, or of the epic in the case of Milton and Homer and Vergil. And this study of the forms of literature would be assisted by, and conducted along with, the study of criticism to which we have previously referred.

Regarded in those wider relations, literature is seen to be a subject of the highest value as an instrument of intellectual culture. Yet at no stage of the school curriculum should this be considered to be its chief value. It is as a humane study, appealing not merely to the intellect but to our whole human nature, that literature excels. If we can lead our pupils to appreciate rightly the literature they read, we shall have achieved what should be our chief aim at all stages of the curriculum. To perceive the beauty of literature, or of any work of art, is implicitly to increase our sympathy with

[1] v. sup. Chap. VI, p. 88.

and reverence for humanity, is to be drawn closer to, and united with, other men. The study of literature is, therefore, in the most literal sense of the word, a *humane* study; and it may be claimed that, regarded thus, as one of "the humanities," it stands *facile princeps* among all the subjects of the school curriculum.

INDEX

For EU product safety concerns, contact us at Calle de José Abascal, 56–1°, 28003 Madrid, Spain or eugpsr@cambridge.org.

www.ingramcontent.com/pod-product-compliance
Ingram Content Group UK Ltd.
Pitfield, Milton Keynes, MK11 3LW, UK
UKHW012331130625
459647UK00009B/217